NETWORKS OF KNOWLEDGE
Collaborative Innovation in International Learning

The network is the pervasive organizational image of the new millennium. This book examines one particular kind of network – the 'knowledge network' – whose primary mandate is to create and disseminate knowledge based on multidisciplinary research that is informed by problem-solving as well as theoretical agendas. In their examination of five knowledge networks based in Canadian universities, and in most cases working closely with researchers in developing countries, the authors demonstrate the ability of networks to cross disciplinary boundaries, to blend the operational with the theoretical, and to respond to broad social processes. Operating through networks, rather than through formal, hierarchical structures, diverse communities of researchers create different kinds of knowledge and disseminate their results effectively across disciplinary, sectoral, and spatial boundaries. Analysis of networks in health, environment, urban, and educational fields suggests that old categories of 'North' and 'South' are becoming blurred, and that the new structures of knowledge creation and dissemination help to sustain collaborative research.

JANICE GROSS STEIN is Professor of Political Science and Director of the Munk Centre for International Studies at the University of Toronto. She specializes in international conflict management, and has acted as a consultant with the Canadian government, the United Nations, and NGOs such as CARE Canada.

RICHARD STREN is Professor of Political Science at the University of Toronto. He has carried out extensive research in Africa on urban planning and politics, and has also coordinated a number of large research networks with colleagues in developing countries.

JOY FITZGIBBON is a doctoral candidate in the Department of Political Science at the University of Toronto.

MELISSA MACLEAN is a doctoral candidate in the Department of Political Science at the University of Toronto.

The Institute of Public Administration of Canada

L'Institut d'administration publique du Canada

The Institute of Public Administration of Canada Series in Public Management and Governance

Editor: Peter Aucoin

This series is sponsored by the Institute of Public Administration of Canada as part of its commitment to encourage research on issues in Canadian public administration, public sector management, and public policy. It also seeks to foster wider knowledge and understanding among practitioners, academics, and the general public.

Networks of Knowledge: Collaborative Innovation in International Learning
Janice Stein, Richard Stren, Joy Fitzgibbon, and Melissa MacLean

The National Research Council in the Innovative Policy Era: Changing Hierarchies, Networks, and Markets
G. Bruce Doern and Richard Levesque

Beyond Service: State Workers, Public Policy, and the Prospects for Democratic Administration
Greg McElligott

Networks of Knowledge

Collaborative Innovation in International Learning

JANICE GROSS STEIN
RICHARD STREN
JOY FITZGIBBON
MELISSA MACLEAN

IPAC
The Institute of
Public Administration of Canada

IAPC
L'Institut d'administration
publique du Canada

UNIVERSITY OF TORONTO PRESS
Toronto Buffalo London

ISBN 0-8020-4844-7 (cloth)
ISBN 0-8020-8371-4 (paper)

Printed on acid-free paper

National Library of Canada Cataloguing in Publication Data

Main entry under title:

Networks of knowledge : collaborative innovation in international learning

Includes bibliographical references and index.
ISBN 0-8020-4844-7 (bound)   ISBN 0-8020-8371-4 (pbk.)

1. Information networks – Canada.   2. Information networks – Ontario –
Toronto – Case studies.   3. Information networks – Nova Scotia – Halifax –
Case studies.   4. Economic development – Research – Canada.
5. Community development – Research – Canada.   6. Communication in
economic development – Canada.   7. Communication in community
development – Canada.   I. Stein, Janice.

HD76.N47 2001   338.91′07′2071   C2001-930320-3

University of Toronto Press acknowledges the financial assistance to its
publishing program of the Canada Council for the Arts and the Ontario
Arts Council.

University of Toronto Press acknowledges the financial support for its publishing activities of the Government of Canada through the Book Publishing
Industry Development Program (BPIDP).

Contents

Preface

This project was created as a response to a Canadian task force established by three leading development organizations – the International Development Research Centre (IDRC), the International Institute for Sustainable Development (IISD), and the North-South Institute – under the leadership of Maurice F. Strong. The purpose of the International Development Research and Policy Task Force was to reflect on Canada's role and position in the twenty-first century, 'and, more specifically, to consider Canadian strengths and capabilities with regard to the global development challenges ahead.' One of the authors of this volume was a member of the task force, whose provocative report, entitled *Connecting with the World: Priorities for Canadian Internationalism in the Twenty-first Century,* was published in 1996.

The report argued that, in an increasingly globalizing world, the challenge to Canada is to build bridges to the developing world 'around issues relating to knowledge and communication for sustainable development' (p. 6). Canada should think of itself as a 'knowledge broker,' with knowledge viewed in three dimensions: the creation of substantive knowledge, in the form of services and products; the creation and maintenance of knowledge-based networks; and the building of the capacity to use, adapt, and build knowledge at the local level (p. 7). While granting that 'the call for "networking" has become a mantra in the 1990s' (p. 9), the task force emphasized that knowledge must have a practical use, since '... in the past far too much knowledge for development has been centralized, generalized, and loaded onto a one-way conveyor belt from North to South, without adequate regard to practical problems, local conditions, or the ultimate end-user. The Task Force [therefore] conceives of a system based on the most up-to-

date communication technologies, that is both dynamic and participatory, where the conveyor belt is multidirectional, and where local
adaptations can be fed back into the system and disseminated more
broadly to other practitioners' (p. 9). To this end, the report recom-
mended funding for the promotion of 'knowledge-based networks' as
a particularly Canadian approach to development.

The task force concluded that universities – at least in Canada – have
played only a minor role in the development of networks. While the
evidence in the report is mixed (there are some examples of successful
university-based networks in the field of development-oriented 'policy
enquiry'), the report's general perspective on universities is that 'the
Canadian academic community ... has not done enough to translate
knowledge into practical tools for sustainable development or useful
instruments for policymakers at home and abroad' (p. 26). We are concerned about the suggestion, implied in the report, that universities are
not active in development. Indeed, our own experience suggests otherwise.

We set out, then, to conduct a preliminary empirical probe into the
contributions that Canadian universities may be making to development networks. We discovered that our universities are indeed making
meaningful and practical contributions to local development efforts
around the globe through network relationships that cross disciplines
and communities. These networks have contributed to the creation of
fascinating, innovative development projects. Sparked by deliberate
strategies that link the best of theory with deeply rooted local experiences, and marked by intellectual creativity and energy, these networks are producing new kinds of knowledge and projects that would
not otherwise be produced. We are left with a series of unanswered
questions that focus, not on *if* universities matter in development, but
rather on *when* and *how*.

Much of the evidence in this book comes from interviews with the
directors and members of the five networks studied: the Canadian
Aging Research Network (CARNET), the Canada International Scientific Exchange Program in Otolaryngology (CISEPO), the Coastal
Resources Research Network (CoRR), the Global Urban Research Initiative (GURI), and the Learning for Environmental Action Program
(LEAP). We are deeply grateful for their willingness to share their
experiences, perspectives, and time. They were generous with all.
None of this research would have been possible without the IDRC and
the Office of the Vice-President, Research and International Relations,

University of Toronto, who provided us with the financial support to pursue the project. We are particularly grateful to Chris Smart at IDRC for his patience and encouragement at each point along the way, and to Heather Munroe-Blum, Vice-President of Research and International Relations at the University of Toronto, for encouraging us to think about this study in the first place, and for her unfailing interest in our subsequent work. We also want to acknowledge the helpful and perceptive comments from anonymous reviewers as well as the support and patience of Virgil Duff, Editor-in-Chief of University of Toronto Press. We are most grateful to Chris Gore, who read the manuscript and provided detailed and insightful suggestions. A very special thank-you goes to our editor Judith Bell, whose painstaking eye for detail and clarity has added so much to this book. She responded to our frequently urgent requests with patience and persistent good humour.

Finally, this book is the result of an extraordinarily fruitful collaboration between faculty and graduate students. The faculty learned an enormous amount from two exceptional graduate students, who became full and valuable contributors in this shared analysis of knowledge networks and international development. The graduate students learned so much from Janice Stein and Richard Stren, and are immensely grateful for the extraordinary opportunity they provided. It was a privilege to learn from them in such an open, supportive, and meaningful collaboration.

Toronto
January 2001

About the Authors

Joy Fitzgibbon is a Ph.D. candidate in political science at the University of Toronto. Her research interests link global politics, public policy, and development with international public health. Her dissertation evaluates the effectiveness of global knowledge networks in the management of tuberculosis. She is currently a Research Assistant in the Munk Centre for International Studies at the University of Toronto.

Melissa MacLean is a Ph.D. candidate in political science at the University of Toronto, currently preparing a thesis on decentralization and democratization in Bolivia. She has worked for the Canadian Council for International Cooperation in Ottawa, the Jesuit Centre for Faith and Social Justice, the Developing Countries Farm Radio Network, both in Toronto, and for a local non-governmental organization in India. She has written and edited numerous popular-format publications on development issues. Her paper 'Canadian Bilateral Aid Policy in Neoliberal Nicaragua' was published by Canada-Americas Policy Alternatives. She has travelled and lived in various parts of South Asia, Latin America, and Europe.

Janice Gross Stein is Director of the Munk Centre for International Studies at the University of Toronto, Harrowston Professor of Conflict Management and Negotiation in the Department of Political Science at the University of Toronto, and a Fellow of the Royal Society of Canada. She received her Ph.D. from McGill University and specializes in international conflict management and development. Her recent publications include *Mean Times: Humanitarian Action in Complex Political Emergencies; Stark Choices, Cruel Dilemmas* (with Michael Bryans and

Bruce D. Jones); *Powder Keg in the Middle East: The Struggle for Gulf Security* (with Geoffrey Kemp); *We All Lost the Cold War* (with Richard Ned Lebow); and *Choosing to Cooperate: How States Avoid Loss* (edited, with Louis W. Pauly).

Richard Stren is Professor of Political Science at the University of Toronto, and former Director of the Centre for Urban and Community Studies. He received his Ph.D. in political science from the University of California at Berkeley. From 1965 to the mid-1990s, he carried out extensive research on African cities, studying urban politics, comparative urban policy, and the effects of international projects on the problems of the urban poor. Since then, his work has turned more toward Latin America and the larger-scale comparative study of urban reform. His major publications include *Housing the Urban Poor in Africa; African Cities in Crisis* (edited, with Rodney White); *Sustainable Cities* (edited, with Rodney White and Joseph Whitney); *The Social Sustainability of Cities* (edited, with Mario Polèse); and *The Challenge of Urban Government* (edited, with Mila Freire). He also edited the four-volume *Urban Research in the Developing World,* published by the Centre for Urban and Community Studies for the Global Urban Research Initiative (GURI), a major international collaborative research project of which he was the Coordinator.

NETWORKS OF KNOWLEDGE

CHAPTER ONE

Knowledge Networks in Global Society: Pathways to Development

Janice Gross Stein and Richard Stren

Introduction

The network is the pervasive organizational image of the new millennium. In our everyday lives, a multitude of networks – communications networks, infrastructure networks, and financial networks, to name only a few – have become central to the way we work and live. In an important comparative study, the sociologist Manuel Castells argues that 'as a historical trend, dominant functions and processes in the information age are increasingly organized around networks. Networks constitute the new social morphology of our societies, and the diffusion of networking logic substantially modifies the operation and outcomes in processes of production, experience, power and culture.'[1] Increasingly, we are living in a networked world.

In this book we examine one particular kind of network – the 'knowledge network' – whose primary mandate is to create and disseminate knowledge. Knowledge, rather than land or capital, has become the most important input of production as the global economy has developed in the post-industrial era. Fortunately, knowledge is a renewable resource, relatively inexpensive to reproduce once the costs of its production have been paid. As we become more aware of the generic importance of networks in the wake of the revolution in information and communication, the special importance of knowledge networks is becoming clear.[2] Knowledge networks are the engine for the interrelated scientific and social processes that have been described as the global 'knowledge revolution.'[3]

We are interested in the complex, subtle, and synergistic relationships between institutions such as universities that generate knowledge in well-understood, well-established ways, and networks that produce knowledge through broader social processes.[4] How 'knowledge-based networks' should be constructed and supported is a central concern of this volume. Within this broader analysis of the origins, contributions, and sustainability of knowledge networks, we focus particularly on the impact of knowledge networks on civil society, both local and global, and on development and development assistance.

Networks that have global reach can draw on sources of knowledge that might otherwise be missed, frame research agendas in response to a broad range of need and expertise, and disseminate the results of research. We argue that there are three important ways in which knowledge networks contribute to innovation and international learning. Knowledge networks:

- produce new knowledge through transdisciplinary research on problems as they are experienced across international boundaries in different contexts;
- produce 'operational' knowledge, acquired through context-bound interactions among multiple sectors of expertise; and
- disseminate knowledge by blurring the boundaries between participants and researchers, thereby ensuring that 'global' knowledge is introduced locally and that 'local' knowledge shapes and, at times, redefines global knowledge.

Our analysis uses university-based networks as exemplars of producers and disseminators of knowledge in a connected world. How important are these networks in the production and dissemination of knowledge? We ask three counterfactual questions: if these networks did not exist, would we know *less*, would we know *differently*, or would we know *more slowly* or *less widely*?[5]

The starting point of this study was the identification of five university-based research networks.[6] Four of these networks were connected to institutions within our own university – the University of Toronto – while a fifth operated through Dalhousie University in Nova Scotia. Our choices were limited by resources and time, but we also wanted to take advantage of the fact that many of our colleagues were willing to share their experiences with us, and that one of us has coordinated a research network for over seven years. The five networks were not chosen as representative cases. We searched for knowledge networks that had been in existence for more than one year, that had some external funding, that were international in scope, and that had kept some records of their objectives, memberships, and processes. We identified four global networks, familiar through their reputations, and included one largely domestic (Canadian) network for purposes of comparison. We make no claims about the representativeness of this group; on the contrary, we consider this analysis of these five networks as a 'first cut,' a preliminary analysis in a field where little systematic evidence exists.[7]

Although the concept of a network is widely used in sociology, organizational behaviour, economics, and comparative public policy, there is little consensus on what a network is. Definitions range from 'everyone you know and everyone who knows you,' a highly contextualized and fluid concept, to 'a map of lines between points,' an explicitly spatial and defined representation.[8] Some sociologists represent all structures as networks, with sets of nodes, or members, and sets of ties, the interconnections between network members.[9] These ties may be formal or informal relationships, transfers, information exchanges, and resource flows between members. This generalized representation of a network does not distinguish sharply enough between hierarchically managed spatial organizations, and horizontal, fluid networks in which members share converging, if passing, interests and exchange resources.

We define a network as a spatially diffuse structure, with no rigidly defined boundaries, consisting of several autonomous nodes sharing common values or interests, linked together in interdependent exchange relationships.[10] Here we are emphasizing the repetitive interactions among members, as well as their converging interests. Another distinguishing characteristic of a network is its largely horizontal, rather than hierarchical, structure. It is this absence of hierarchy which gives networks their flexibility, their capacity to expand and contract in response to changing environments, and their potential to adapt.[11]

Another approach to defining a network is to compare it with other dominant organizational protocols. The most important alternative modalities are markets and hierarchies. Walter Powell argues that networks can be clearly distinguished from both markets and hierarchies:

> In market transactions the benefits to be exchanged are clearly specified, no trust is required, and agreements are bolstered by the power of legal sanction. Network forms of exchange, however, entail indefinite, sequential transactions within the context of a general pattern of interaction. Sanctions are typically normative rather than legal. The value of the

goods to be exchanged in markets are much more important than the relationship itself; when relations do matter, they are frequently defined as if they were commodities. In hierarchies, communication occurs in the context of the employment contract. Relationships matter and previous interactions shape current ones, but the patterns and context of intra-organizational exchange are most strongly shaped by one's position within the formal hierarchical structure of authority.[12]

In contrast to markets, relationships matter in networks. The distinction between markets and networks, some have argued, is overdrawn since relationships matter in markets as well, and networks are systems of exchange, as are markets. What is different in knowledge networks is the nature of what is being exchanged and the relationships that develop around the 'exchange' and the deepening of knowledge as the basic commodity.[13]

In contrast to hierarchies, flows in networks are predominantly horizontal rather than vertical. These kinds of flows are especially important when new knowledge is at a premium. 'The most useful information is rarely that which flows down the formal chain of command in an organization, or that which can be inferred from shifting price signals. Rather, it is that which is obtained from someone whom you have dealt with in the past and found to be reliable ... The open-ended, relational features of networks, with their relative absence of explicit quid pro quo behavior, greatly enhance the ability to transmit and learn new knowledge and skills.'[14]

An absence of hierarchy creates many advantages but also challenges. When largely horizontal networks are established, how is membership determined? How are 'nodes' created? We have little systematic evidence about how knowledge networks, our particular interest, begin and about the processes that define these networks. Are there boundaries around the membership or is the network infinitely expandable? Are there rules of inclusion and exclusion? If there are rules, how are they made and how stable are they? In short, how formal are networks?

These questions are relevant to knowledge networks, a subset of generic networks and the focus of this study. Ronnie Lipschutz defines a global knowledge network as the actors and linkages among these actors that transcend boundaries and localities.[15] Global knowledge networks create and transfer knowledge – scientific, community-based, and policy-relevant – as well as the necessary hardware and finances to support knowledge acquisition and implementation. This transfer between scientific knowledge, local community-based knowledge, and policy-relevant knowledge is a process of 'social learning.' Such knowledge networks operate within a globally shared system of knowledge creation and transmission, while the practices of individual members are informed by the histories, politics, and ecologies of the national and local places in which they work; in this sense, global knowledge networks link the global, the national, and the local. Lipschutz finds considerable internal hierarchy within the networks, reflecting imbalances in resources of network members.[16]

A recent study of knowledge networks in Canada similarly develops a concept of 'formal' knowledge networks that seems to have many of the attributes of highly structured, hierarchical organizations. While he recognizes what he calls 'open networks,' which are set up in order to create new knowledge with no concerns 'about possible applications or development,' Howard Clark appears to favour what he calls 'development networks,' whose members and projects 'are carefully chosen by peer review using criteria based on excellence. The network exists to create new knowledge, but also to accelerate the application of that new knowledge to economic or social development. The network has a tight form of governance, a formal constitution, and a more hierarchical structure.'[17] As this study shows, knowledge-based networks need not be, and often are not, so tightly conceived and organized.

Knowledge networks do more than link nodes and transfer knowledge. Economists consider these networks as private producers of public goods who add value. A knowledge network is 'a set of activities undertaken by discrete autonomous actors endowed with knowledge producing and consuming capacity ... that increase the value of the activities of the actors, contribute to the expansion of knowledge, broaden the scope for the applications of new knowledge, and enable knowledge-feedback and development.'[18] Members of a knowledge network actively participate in the exchange of information, in contrast to information or 'broadcasting' networks, in which the roles of sender and receiver are clearly demarcated. This participation adds value for the users by improving the knowledge that is shared.

We define knowledge networks as spatially diffuse structures, often aggregations of individuals and organizations, linked together by shared interest in and concern about a puzzling problem. These individuals and organizations are autonomous, but coalesce to generate and add to knowledge about the shared problem. Knowledge networks generally have no rigidly defined boundaries, and share knowledge across political and social boundaries.

Knowledge is traditionally shared through copying already established knowledge generated in a hierarchy; this is equivalent to a process of 'knowledge free-riding,' so common, for example, in peasant agriculture.[19] Alternatively, knowledge can be shared through 'pooling': no one agent has encompassing knowledge, but different agents who have different pieces or kinds of knowledge come together to share through active participation and exchange. Copying requires a less active process than pooling, and, indeed, varieties of pooling characterize knowledge networks. Pooling works best when a network is diverse. Members can bring different pieces to the table and add value, either by improving the likelihood of solving the puzzle, or by enabling different members to use information for different purposes. In either case, the stock of knowledge is augmented.

Michael Gibbons, in an important analysis of the 'new production' of knowledge within networks, argues that the new mode differs in almost every important respect from the familiar, institutionally grounded, scientific mode of knowledge production characteristic of the last century. Knowledge networks increasingly operate within a context of application: problems are set within a transdisciplinary rather than a unidisciplinary framework, and research is carried out in non-hierarchical, heterogeneously organized forms which are essentially transient rather than permanent.[20] Knowledge networks involve the close interaction of many partners throughout the process, and consequently the process and the knowledge that is created are more socially accountable. These networks, Gibbons argues, are 'socially distributed knowledge production schemes,' where knowledge is disseminated by those who are its active producers.[21] In this context, evaluation of knowledge is expanding beyond traditional peer review to include additional criteria such as usefulness and the inclusion of a community of practitioners in the judgment of quality.

This argument that processes of knowledge production are undergoing fundamental transition has been deeply contested. Critics insist that, at most, transformation applies largely to 'scientific' knowledge that can be commodified in the larger marketplace. Indeed, careful analysis of the evidence supplied by Gibbons and his colleagues finds little empirical support beyond the workings of scientific research that travels to the broader marketplace. Our analysis of five knowledge networks that draw heavily on social science, rather than basic science, supports the argument that processes of knowledge creation are being transformed in important ways across disciplines, well beyond the sciences.

We examine the *significance* of knowledge networks. We want to explore whether they contribute, and if they do, what kind of contribution they make to the development and sharing of knowledge across spaces of all kinds. Insofar as knowledge networks bring participants together across space and time and, often, across cultures, they create opportunities to partner, exchange ideas, collaborate on the identification of problems, and parcel out research responsibilities. In the process, knowledge networks have the potential to contribute to the definition of problems, the shaping of the research agenda, the execution of research, and the dissemination of results. University-led knowledge networks provide an ideal basis for a preliminary assessment of whether and where, in the chain of knowledge generation, production, and dissemination, networks contribute.

Once knowledge networks, defined by their shared commitment to develop and expand knowledge, are established, how are they managed? How extensive is the membership and how dense is the interaction among members? It may well be more appropriate, given the non-hierarchical and fluid structure of networks, to examine, not how they are managed, but rather how they are governed. How, for example, are entitlements and responsibilities established? How are the most important decisions made? If global knowledge networks are only loosely governed, how are they sustained over time? Indeed, some would question whether sustainability over time is an appropriate criterion for a flexible and fluid horizontal structure of exchange relationships that is constantly adapting to a changing environment. It may be that the comparative advantage of knowledge networks, in comparison to their more fixed counterparts, is their capacity to come and go. Analysis of the structure and governance of these five knowledge networks sheds light on important boundary issues: new and broader boundaries may suggest that traditional patterns of international institutional collaboration are changing, or that new processes of knowledge creation and dissemination are driving the reconfiguration of boundaries.

We begin with a brief profile of each of the five knowledge networks that we examine in this volume, including their origins and objectives. We then compare them in terms of their governance, patterns of coordination and decision-making, criteria for membership, the research they have conducted, the knowledge they have shared, and their sustainability in the shadow of states and markets. In the next chapter, we grapple with the difficult conceptual and practical problems of measuring and assessing the effectiveness of knowledge networks, consider the relationship of global networks to more established, hierarchical organizations, and assess the contributions that knowledge networks can make to development and development assistance.

Profiles of Networks

The Canada International Scientific Exchange Program in Otolaryngology (CISEPO) is based in the Department of Otolaryngology at Mount Sinai Hospital, a teaching hospital affiliated with the University of Toronto. Begun as an exchange program between Canada and Israel, CISEPO now operates with academic partners in seven continents. Its mission is twofold: to enrich academic medicine and health care in Canada and internationally, through joint medical research, education, and collaboration across borders and disciplines, and to use areas of shared scientific concern to promote peace-building in regions of the world prone to violent conflict.

The Coastal Resources Research Network (CoRR), which grew out of ten independent research projects on mollusc culture, all funded by the International Development Research Centre (IDRC) in Ottawa, conducts interdisciplinary research on mollusc culture and aquaculture, and their effects on coastal communities. Initially dedicated to biotechnical research, CoRR gradually expanded to include an interdisciplinary focus on community-related social and economic issues. The focus changed in response to community feedback from earlier phases of network activity. The network is based in Dalhousie University in Halifax, Nova Scotia, with partners in Asia, Africa, and the Caribbean.

The Global Urban Research Initiative (GURI), funded originally by the Urban Poverty Program of the Ford Foundation and coordinated from the Centre for Urban and Community Studies at the University of Toronto, became the largest global urban research network. It was created in response to the need of the Foundation to develop a better understanding of urban issues so that its programs could be better informed. A central objective of the network was to strengthen the professional skills and institutional position of local researchers. The fundamental premise of GURI was that 'developing-country researchers are uniquely qualified to interpret global forces in their own local context and to transmit their understanding of their local environment to the outside world.'[22] It brought together leading urbanists in twelve subregions in Africa, Asia, and Latin America to work on policy-relevant urban issues and to discuss and disseminate their findings through meetings, workshops, international conferences, and the publication of research papers and books.

The Learning for Environmental Action Program (LEAP), coordinated by the University of Toronto's Ontario Institute for Studies in Education (OISE), is an ongoing program of the International Council for Adult Education (ICAE). It arose from an international meeting of adult educators who felt that adult education had failed to grapple adequately with environmental issues. The network was given official status by the ICAE, through the creation and funding of a program on adult education. The central purpose of the network is to develop theories and strategies for environmental adult education, with a primary focus on making connections between theory and practice. To make these connections, LEAP is committed to raising awareness of environmental issues within the adult education sector; making links with environmental organizations and community groups to help strengthen the educational component of their work by incorporating adult education; and strengthening links between knowledge created in the community and that created in the universities. The network operates in all major regions of the world.

The Canadian Aging Research Network (CARNET) is the only one of our case-study networks to operate largely within national borders. It was established at the University of Toronto as part of a program of centres of excellence funded by the Canadian federal government in 1990, and when it completed its mandate in 1996, it chose not to apply for a renewal of its funding. We include it in this study as a case of a self-terminating network, and examine why members chose not to continue. CARNET was a partnership among federal granting agencies, universities, corporations, research institutes, and federal and provincial governments. The network included twenty-four researchers from ten universities and one private firm. CARNET's purpose was to analyse the social implications of an aging population and to outline their consequences for the individual, the community, business, and industry. In the process of its research, the network was to establish partnerships between researchers and the wider community, especially the business community, and to provide education and develop research opportunities for young scholars.

Governance and Boundaries

Governance of autonomous or independent members connected principally through shared values and exchange relationships is, at first glance, almost an oxymoron. Yet, some form of governance in knowledge networks is necessary to permit coordination on research priorities, planning of research and dissemination strategies, and accountability to funders.[23] Governance structures have received relatively little attention in the analysis of knowledge networks, which are characteristically nimble, flexible, and possibly transient. The challenge is to develop a pattern of governance that provides for coordination and accountability, but does not compromise either the autonomy of members to draw on local resources to generate and shape knowledge, or members' flexibility to reshape agendas. These are among the strongest assets that knowledge networks have.

The governance patterns of the five networks vary in their degree of centralization and formal structure. We defined a network as a spatially diffuse organization, without sharply specified boundaries, consisting of several relatively autonomous nodes, linked together in interdependent exchange relationships. These exchange relationships can radiate out from a core to the nodes, in a relatively centralized structure. In the archetype centralized network, although the core seeks extensive input from members, it determines the agenda, establishes whatever rules may exist for new members, and sets the criteria of accountability to outside funders. This kind of network functions as a 'hub' with 'spokes.'

In a decentralized network, each node relates directly to the others as well as to the core. Members operate with a great deal of autonomy in the management and reporting of funds, and the reporting requirements and evaluation are frequently informal rather than formal. The 'structure' of the network may remain unspecified, and meetings are likely to be ad hoc. There is no formal structure of governance. In a 'fishnet,' or very decentralized structure, no core exists at all; links go in every direction among all the nodes.

None of our networks matched the pure 'fishnet' model; all had a central coordinator, but the five knowledge networks varied considerably in the degree of centralization. LEAP, funded by an international council, was the most decentralized network with the most autonomous nodes, followed closely by CISEPO; CoRR was somewhat more structured, and GURI even more so. The domestic network, CARNET, was the most centralized network with the funder directly involved in governance.

The LEAP network is divided into seven regions, which span the globe.[24] The approximately 1,500 organizations and individuals who have asked to be added to the mailing list for LEAP's newsletter are all considered to be members. In this sense, the network has no fixed boundaries. The core of the network, however, is the group of regional and subregional coordinators who represent organizations affiliated with ICAE.

Each region's involvement with the LEAP network is coordinated by an unpaid, volunteer representative of an environmental or adult education non-governmental organization (NGO), institute, or university that is in turn associated with ICAE. Consultation is lateral, rather than through the centre in a 'hub' and 'spoke' process. Regional coordinators try to meet once a year to define future directions and exchange ideas for project development. Regional coordinators and their organizations also choose the central or interregional coordinator, who, over time, has made considerable contributions of services in kind to the maintenance of the network.[25] As we shall see, the contribution made by the coordinators of all five networks is critical. In LEAP, however, the position of the coordinator has been sufficiently institutionalized that a successful transition has occurred from one member to another.

The decision-making culture in LEAP appears to be informal, based on extensive consultation, consensus, and a high degree of trust among the coordinators. While routine management issues are left to the interregional coordinator, the definition of long-term strategies, the shaping of international initiatives, and the development of special projects are the product of extensive consultation among the regional and interregional coordinators. It is likely that this decentralized, horizontal structure evolved in part because of the part-time status of the interregional coordinator and the strong institutional bases of the regional coordinators.

CISEPO is less consensual in style. Its processes are stamped by the strong leadership of the founding director and a formalized structure of governance, but the director tends to work through consensus, respect the autonomy of project directors, and delegate authority and accountability. Members are chosen carefully by the director and his partners from leading researchers worldwide, on the basis of their scientific leadership but also for their cultural sensitivity and their capacity to contribute to peace-building. The network now has approximately fifty core members, one hundred peripheral members, and an additional hundred and fifty interested associates. It is the director, however, who chooses new members and partners; the network does have boundaries as well as a formal governance structure. The network reports to a board of directors, which includes representatives from the family foundation which provided the initial funding, the coordinator, and his two business partners.[26]

The GURI network was more centralized, with explicit procedures and a reasoned order to its processes. It was organized into four large regions, each with a regional coordinator drawn from, and based in, the region. These large regions were further divided into subregions, each with its own coordinator (or node). There were twelve nodes in the network, as well as the central coordinator and his team. The majority of the members were academic researchers connected to universities, but some were associated with research institutes. The considerable diversity of members of GURI was both a real strength in shaping research agendas and a challenge to the core team. Despite the scope of its diversity, however, GURI was a bounded network; members were chosen by the core team, in extensive consultation with the funder and the other coordinators, on the basis of specific skills and attributes.

CARNET, the only network without nodes across national borders, although it did have members in the United States as well as Canada, was the most highly centralized. The network consisted of twenty-four principal investigators from ten universities across Canada, and one consulting firm. Most of the principal investigators designed cross-disciplinary and multi-institutional projects. In this network, as well, members were chosen by the director, in close consultation with other principal investigators.

The network was governed by a tri-council directorate composed of the three governmental granting agencies; a steering committee, comprising representatives from member universities, partner corporations, research institutes, and all the participating levels of governments, which provided advice; and a management committee, which addressed routine research issues. The management committee included the directors of the four research groups, who were in turn advised by business representatives from partner organizations. A central coordinating unit, a research institute within one of the universities, provided the infrastructure and facilitated communication.[27] The criteria for the evaluation of the network products, processes, and strategic development were set by the government funding program in advance, and the network provided detailed annual reports to the tri-council directorate in accordance with these requirements. Research directors similarly provided regular detailed reports to the director, who needed this information to meet formal reporting requirements. These were onerous and not always tied to project goals. They became a significant transaction cost, as the directorate required increasingly greater amounts of information. As one network member observed, 'The reporting requirements were a major negative. There were liter-ally dozens of forms. The ridiculous amount of reporting served no purpose and did not further research goals.'[28]

Our examination of these five knowledge networks shows variation in boundaries, structure, and governance. Membership in the net-works varied in its fluidity. In two (CoRR and LEAP), a subscription to the newsletter was sufficient for organizational or individual member-ship. In both these cases, however, core researchers from each of the projects formed the basis of the network. In the other three, rules for membership were set by core teams, usually in consultation with other members, and by funders. These knowledge networks *were largely bounded on the basis of expertise.*

Networks varied as well in their structures. The variance in central-ization and in the explicitness of procedures of accountability was in part a function of the directors and their management style, in part a function of funders and their reporting requirements, and in part a function of the institutional connections which undergirded the net-works and provided support. In three of the five cases, the networks closely approximated horizontal structures that were responsive to members' needs as well as knowledge. In the fourth case, GURI, the director's management style softened and mediated the donor's reporting requirements. In CARNET, although, as we shall see, the net-work generated significant research results, its hierarchical structure and bureaucratic processes defeated the interest of the research com-munities engaged in the processes. It seems that members of knowl-edge networks value the horizontal structure and flexible procedures. Even though they were not generally fluid, these knowledge networks were flexible.

Networks and Public Policy

One of the important ways in which Canadian universities work with partners in developing countries is through knowledge-based networks. This should not be surprising, given the fact that universities are themselves centrally engaged in the creation and dissemination of knowledge and that the *modus operandi* of university researchers is to work with other colleagues in a peer-oriented, collaborative fashion. Most major research which eventually gets published is reviewed, usually anonymously, by committees of peers, research journals are voluntarily managed by committees of peers in traditional disciplines or areas of study, and universities themselves operate largely on a democratic and transparent basis. To this structural predisposition to horizontal, non-authoritarian relationships should be added the recent tendency to privilege new forms of development based on networks rather than on hierarchical relationships.

This trend toward networks as the organizational basis of development reflects two important tendencies in the public policy-making field. The first is the emergence, when important policy issues are being discussed, of what can be called 'policy communities' – or groups of recognized experts in particular fields – operating between the public and private sectors, often between countries. These policy communities are not organized groups, but are based on network relationships, and come together in response to particular challenges. Academics are often members of these communities, but so are NGO activists, government officials, consultants, and elected officials with an immediate interest in global policy problems.[29] At the international level, these groups have been called 'epistemic communities.'[30] In local policy communities, however, the same individuals may play different roles at different times; for example, a university professor may be an ex-minister or former municipal councillor, may consult for an international agency, and may be active in a local NGO. This overlap of policy roles – typically involving academics – is particularly visible in developing countries, where academic salaries and conditions of work are insecure, requiring professionals to protect themselves through multiple sources of income and employment.[31] Policy communities cohere through networking in response to situational factors, rather than through common membership in bounded organizations.[32]

A second, and complementary, tendency is the gradual shift from 'bureaucratic' models of organization to what have been called 'post-bureaucratic' models. If the bureaucratic model of organization is based on efficiency, administration, control, and adherence to rules and procedures as key objectives, the post-bureaucratic model is oriented toward quality and value, demand rather than supply, production, achieving agreement on norms, and understanding and joint problem-solving within a group.[33]

These current trends have proximate institutional origins. As Hugh Heclo observed, the trend toward 'government by remote control' in the United States began in the 1970s in the context of a paradox of expanding governmental functions and budgets, together with a relatively stable bureaucratic complement at the national level. Partly as a result of limited personnel resources, but strengthened by tendencies of increasing complexity and specialization in policy-making, 'issue networks' developed, based on policy professionals and 'highly knowledgeable policy-watchers.'[34] In the developing world, this shift to a less hierarchical policy model has coincided with the reform of the centralized state, an ongoing process which over time is reducing large bureaucratic organizations, decentralizing social functions to both smaller local government agencies and private sector firms, and developing closer links with civil society organizations. Both of these tendencies devalue hierarchy and strengthen horizontal relations, and both require a rich knowledge-based environment to function successfully.

The organization of the networks discussed in this volume reflects these attributes. Most of the networks are made up of like-minded professionals, operating out of many different locations at the same time, who share a common policy or research goal. An open, democratic decision-making process characterizes all of them. Since the network itself generally accounts for only a small part of its members' overall resource commitment or income base, network activities must be negotiated in order to find a 'fit' with the members' other activities.

In the case of CISEPO, for example, most members operate within the related fields of otolaryngology, oncology, radiology, epidemiology, cardiology, and molecular biology. The work involves research and training as well as clinical care. Businessmen as well as medical professionals make up the board of directors; and the network is active in Canada, Israel, Jordan, and the Palestinian Authority. The administrative structure of the network is sparse, and relies heavily on ties of friendship and the personal efforts of the Toronto coordinator. But the core funding is relatively limited in relation to the scope of the network's activities, with the result that CISEPO tries to 'piggyback' on other grants and activities whenever possible.

CoRR is also an interdisciplinary network. It grew out of ten separate projects funded by a single donor – IDRC – and, while originally the network was based on biological research, it shifted after 1992 to more community-based, social science research on the premise that the coastal communities involved in the network needed to develop a more long-term framework for sustainability and equity. Coordinated by a Dalhousie University biologist, with a research associate and an administrative assistant, the project works with communities in Sri Lanka, India, Indonesia, Malaysia, Gambia, Sudan, Jamaica, and the Philippines. Although it is more hierarchical than most and given more direction by the major donor agency, its activities are diverse and its range has been wide for more than a decade.

The GURI project, the best funded in our group of case studies, was also organized around a major interdisciplinary area, urban planning and research in the developing world. It operated in twelve core countries – Chile, Brazil, the Dominican Republic, El Salvador, Mexico, Morocco, Egypt, Tanzania, South Africa, India, Bangladesh, and the Philippines. Only about half its key local researchers were full-time academics, and one-third of the Southern research groups were organized around NGOs rather than academic institutions. The selection of themes for research and other related activities was, after the network's first phase ended in 1993, consistently carried out through majority vote, irrespective of the preferences of the Northern coordinators. The major donor accepted these choices, even when a chosen project overlapped with a major project supported by another branch of the same foundation. The ability of the Southern members of the network to work in an area of their own choice added to their commitment to the project.

The LEAP network is the least 'bureaucratic' of the five knowledge networks, in part because of its origins and in part because of its organizational form. LEAP was created in the late 1980s by adult educators connected to a major international NGO – the ICAE. The ICAE had already spawned, in 1977, the International Participatory Research Network, whose first coordinator was very explicit about the organizational principles involved:

We deliberately chose the concept of a network for our organizational form. We had discussed ideas such as an international project, an organization, an association, a research council of some kind and other organizational forms. We wanted a structure which was horizontal in power terms, which allowed for and encouraged autonomous locally or regionally accountable nodes, which took the cues from the grass roots rather than the centre, and where power flowed according to the tasks at hand rather than funding, tradition, or imperial world divisions ... We were among the first groups to develop and make use consciously of the concept of networking, an organizational form which has since become a nearly universal model for global collaboration.[35]

While LEAP is committed to linking environmental themes to adult education programs at the community level, it also supports research and works with university departments of adult education around the world. It has the widest geographic reach of the five networks, but only a single coordinator to work with the regional coordinators.

At the other end of the organizational spectrum, representing a much more centralized and 'bureaucratic' network, is CARNET, the second-best funded network among our cases. A considerable degree of centralization was implicit from the outset, since the project was closely advised by a directorate representing the three federal government donors and a steering committee. A management committee dealt with day-to-day research issues, but even this committee was made up of four research directors, advised by business representatives. The centre also signed formal contracts with the researchers and required detailed annual reports. The funders' reporting requirements eventually became so onerous that the researchers – who had achieved considerable success in their substantive work – decided not to reapply for a second round of funding. In addition, the network never succeeded in breaking down disciplinary boundaries between the sociologists and the psychologists within the ten participating universities.

Analysis of these five cases suggests two major conclusions. First, to be successful, a network must afford the project leader or coordinator a *sufficient degree of freedom and flexibility* to make strategic choices in collaboration with the whole group, free of unnecessary 'bureaucratic' restrictions. Relatively open networks with a minimum of centralized structure seem to encourage innovation and cross-disciplinary collaboration. The degree of centralization seems to be in part a function of the level of funding, and the reporting and implementation requirements of the funders. More flexible and horizontal relationships are more likely when there is more than a single funder and different members of the network receive funding at different times.

Second, *a great deal of variation in organizational structure and style is possible*, even among research networks connected to universities. Organizational styles differ according to funders' requirements, the explicitness of objectives, and the production of 'deliverables,' but they also vary according to the 'organizational culture' of the specialized work, the relative importance of NGOs in the network and – perhaps most important – the personal styles of the network leaders. Since research networks are, almost by definition, accretions of small groups of professionals who relate well to each other and who gain additional energy by working together, they develop a 'personality' which gives a certain quality to their work, with which they all identify. E-mail, fax, and other media of electronic communication undoubtedly help the networks to function, but they do not guarantee commitment and continuity. Our analysis shows that personal, face-to-face meetings, either as a group, or between the coordinator and the network members, are essential to keep networks operating in an effective fashion. These personal relationships tend to reinforce the specific character of individual networks and the commitment of members.

It is an open question whether these 'informal' elements of network operation can function in a complementary fashion with the often bureaucratic requirements of international donors. The flexible support and direction that networks require to function at their most productive level must fit, however, with donor expectations if networks are to fulfil their potential and flourish. We return to this question in chapter 8.

University-based Networks and Knowledge Production

We argue that the knowledge-based research networks examined in this volume make three kinds of contribution to processes of knowledge production: they generate new knowledge; they generate 'operational' knowledge; and they disseminate global knowledge locally. The first contribution is a function of the interdisciplinary quality of the networks we have selected. The second is related to the mixture of academic and non-academic work that the networks perform. And the third is related to the constant interaction between distant colleagues and global disciplines, on the one hand, and local activities, on the other. These three qualities of interdisciplinarity, operationality, and contextualization are each important to the production of knowledge.

These three qualities of research networks parallel important trends in the global redefinition of knowledge production. Processes of knowledge production are changing, in part in response to changes in the patterns and speed of the communication of information, and in part in response to an evolving social and economic context.

Responding to these changes, organizations have explicitly embraced the notion of the 'learning organization.' The approach builds on the experience of successful American companies, but also on earlier work in organizational learning theory by psychologist Chris Argyris, planner Donald Schon, and the physicist David Bohm.[36] Peter Senge, in his widely read book *The Fifth Discipline*, stresses the importance of self-reinforcing learning in organizations, enabling employees, working together in teams, to respond rapidly to new signals and trends in the marketplace.[37] A major element in this approach is an emphasis on research, since relevant and rapidly accessible knowledge produces major benefits.[38] To access and use this knowledge effectively, organizations must decentralize by 'moving decisions down the organizational hierarchy; designing business units where, to the greatest degree possible, local decision makers confront the full range of issues and dilemmas intrinsic in growing and sustaining any business enterprise.'[39]

The increasing emphasis on information-gathering, research, and 'learning' within organizations is broadening traditional concepts of 'knowledge production.'[40] Lisa Peattie develops a concept of 'operational knowledge' as a combination of the general principles derived from rigorous comparative study of cases, on the one hand, and practical technique and experience, on the other.[41] General principles of human action are applied to specific local circumstances. Policy conclusions from case studies draw on comparative case evidence to develop general recommendations.

The argument that dense, textured local case studies are a valuable part of a strategy for developing more effective operational knowledge has much in common with analyses of the benefits of knowledge-based networks of research. Research networks add value by enabling a continuous interaction between policies and issues that are important in a local context, and concepts and ideas that have broader, comparative currency. Given the broad mandate of international agencies to promote multidimensional aspects of development, combined with the tendency among academic researchers and writers to seek approaches and strategies that can successfully be transposed from one environment to another, systematic local information on the application of concepts and hypotheses in different settings is especially valuable. Networks can help to establish the parameters for these controlled comparisons, since they are flexible enough to permit researchers in very different local situations to validate local experience in the light of more general concepts, and they have sufficient structure to make cross-cultural comparisons and experiments possible.

A significant recent study of urban planning in Denmark makes the important point that the rationality of plans and planning is always refined when plans are applied locally. Thus, plans or planning approaches that seem rational in one context, or on the basis of universal principles of justice and sustainability, almost inevitably are contextualized when attempts are made to put them into practice. The result is a particular institutional mix that owes as much or more to local ideas of what is both right and possible, as it does to more abstract concepts and principles.[42] Institutional forms and procedures, often lauded as 'best practices' in one setting, may founder or be radically transformed in the process of application in another setting. Pierre Bourdieu argues that the applications of formal models to real-life situations are likely to go awry, since 'theoretical knowledge constructed by the social scientist is fundamentally different from the practical knowledge employed by actors.'[43] Yet, as Bourdieu cogently argues, it is practical knowledge, or practices, that ought to be the subject of study.[44]

Increasingly, knowledge is produced in the developing world by researchers – located in universities, independent centres, or NGOs – who work in networks, with colleagues in other disciplines, in other places, in different kinds of institutions on subjects that are defined according to their practical importance rather than their disciplinary interest. The process of knowledge creation is becoming more and more heterogeneous rather than homogeneous, transdisciplinary rather than disciplinary, and 'operational' as well as abstract. In the next chapter, we examine the contribution that knowledge networks make to this expanded concept of knowledge production.

NOTES

1 Manuel Castells, *The Rise of the Network Society,* Vol. 1 of *The Information Age: Economy, Society and Culture* (Oxford: Blackwell, 1996), 469. See also *Networks in the Global Village,* ed. Barry Wellman (Boulder: Westview Press, 1999).
2 See, in particular, the report of the International Development Research and Policy Task Force, *Connecting with the World: Priorities for Canadian Inter-*

nationalism in the Twenty-first Century (Ottawa and Winnipeg: International Development Research Centre, International Institute for Sustainable Development, North-South Institute, 1996).

3 See Graciela Chichilnisky, 'The Knowledge Revolution,' *Journal of International Trade and Economic Development* 7, no. 1 (March 1998): 39–45.

4 The Strong task force concluded that universities – at least in Canada – have played only a minor role in the development of networks. While the evidence in the report is mixed (there are some examples in an Annex of successful university-based networks in the field of development-oriented 'policy enquiry'), the report's general perspective on universities is that 'the Canadian academic community ... has not done enough to translate knowledge into practical tools for sustainable development or useful instruments for policymakers at home and abroad' (p. 26). Apart from what we may think about the (apparent) self-referential position of the task force on where responsibility lies for translating knowledge into action, and for responding to the 'sustainable development' challenge, we are concerned about the implied suggestion that universities are not active in development. Indeed, our own experience suggests otherwise.

5 We provide some operational measures for each of these counterfactual questions in the second part of the analysis.

6 The case studies – chapters 3 to 7 – of the five networks were carried out by two doctoral candidates, Melissa MacLean and Joy Fitzgibbon. Richard Stren assigned the case study of his own network to MacLean, who in turn indicated to the network members that they would be cited anonymously unless they expressly waived this privilege. Work on the case studies of the four other networks was divided between Fitzgibbon and MacLean. Because four of the networks were coordinated at the University of Toronto, Fitzgibbon and MacLean had access to records, papers, and some of the active administrators. For more information, they carried out telephone or e-mail interviews, and also examined materials received through the mail.

7 The degree to which systematic information about development networks is lacking is reflected in the selection of networks for analysis in another study – in this case, a monograph by Howard C. Clark of the International Institute for Sustainable Development, entitled *Formal Knowledge Networks: A Study of Canadian Experiences* (Winnipeg: International Institute for Sustainable Development, 1998). Clark's monograph, which, like the present study, takes up some of the issues raised by the Strong task force, bases its findings on interviews and other information from twenty-seven formal

Canadian networks. While Clark's work was carried out independently from ours, not one of the networks that we investigated is mentioned in his study.

8 Jessica Lipnack and Jeffrey Stamps, *The Networking Book: People Connecting with People* (New York: Routledge and Kegan Paul, 1986), 2.

9 Barry Wellman and S.D. Berkowitz, 'Introduction: Studying Social Structures,' in *Social Structures: A Network Approach*, ed. Barry Wellman and S.D. Berkowitz (Cambridge: Cambridge University Press, 1988), 4.

10 A similar definition is that of Lipnack and Stamps: 'A network is a web of free-standing participants cohering through shared values and interests. Networks are composed of self-reliant people and of independent groups' (p. 4). For related concepts, see Kathryn Sikkink, 'Human Rights, Principled Issue Networks, and Sovereignty in Latin America,' *International Organization* 47, no. 3 (Summer 1993): 411–41; and Paul Wapner, 'Politics beyond the State: Environmental Activism and World Civic Politics,' *World Politics* 47 (April 1995): 311–40. Sikkink defines networks as 'groups who share common norms and goals, and exchange information, services and funds through dense webs of interconnections.'

11 Castells, *Rise of the Network Society.*

12 Walter W. Powell, 'Neither Market nor Hierarchy: Network Forms of Organization,' *Organizational Behavior* 12 (1990): 301–2.

13 Pierre Bourdieu, in *Homo Academicus* (Stanford: Stanford University Press, 1988), demonstrates the importance of markets in academic systems and distinguishes between 'cultural capital' and 'academic capital.'

14 Ibid., 304.

15 Ronnie D. Lipschutz with Judith Mayer, *Global Civil Society and Global Environmental Governance* (New York: State University of New York Press, 1996).

16 Lipschutz, *Global Civil Society,* 73–6.

17 Clark, *Formal Knowledge Networks,* 10.

18 Nazli Choucri and Steven R.L. Millman, *Knowledge Networks* (Cambridge, MA: MIT Technology and Development Program, 1998).

19 Paul Collier, *Social Capital and Poverty,* Social Capital Initiative Working Paper 4 (Washington, DC: World Bank, 1998), 8–9.

20 Michael Gibbons et al., *New Production of Knowledge: Dynamics of Science and Research in Contemporary Societies* (London: Sage, 1994).

21 Ibid., 10.

22 GURI document.

23 To the extent that a network builds in a capacity for authoritative decision-making, it acquires the more formal status of a 'club.' See Collier, *Social Capital and Poverty,* 18–19.

24 The seven regions are Asia/South Pacific, the Caribbean, Latin America, North America, Europe, Africa, and the Middle East.

25 The present coordinator is a doctoral student who was working on a dissertation on environmental adult education. Her academic work and her work for LEAP were consequently closely linked. This kind of voluntary contribution is typical rather than unusual in many of the networks.

26 The board consists of fifteen members, half of whom are drawn from the medical community, the other half from the broader community. All are non-sectarian with international interests.

27 The Institute for Human Development, Life Course, and Aging at the University of Toronto was the coordinating unit.

28 Interview, Dr Fergus Craik, 25 August 1997.

29 Wolfgang Reinicke and Francis Deng, *Critical Choices: The United Nations, Networks, and the Future of Global Governance* (Ottawa: IDRC, 2000).

30 Our use of the concept of policy community is closely related to, but distinct from, 'epistemic communities,' or transnational communities of experts who share a consensus on causal beliefs and on policy-relevant knowledge. Extensive research has been done, for example, on the environmental and arms control epistemic communities and their impact on policy. These communities are informal, often with no clearly elaborated structure, no explicit criteria for membership, and no systematic pattern of funding. Moreover, they share an expert consensus. Knowledge networks, as we conceive them, do not necessarily share an expert consensus or agree on policy-relevant knowledge. They are formed in part to examine causal patterns; in this sense, they can be considered as precursors to possible epistemic communities. They differ as well from epistemic communities in their structures. They are self-declared networks, with a structure, a pattern of governance, and a set of boundaries.

    For analysis of epistemic communities, see Ernest Haas, *When Knowledge Is Power* (Berkeley: University of California Press, 1990); Peter M. Haas, 'Introduction: Epistemic Communities and International Policy Coordination,' in special issue on 'Knowledge, Power, and International Policy Coordination,' ed. Peter M. Haas, *International Organization* 46, no. 1 (Winter 1992): 1–35; and Emmanuel Adler, 'The Emergence of Cooperation: National Epistemic Communities and the International Evolution of the Idea of Arms Control,' *International Organization* 46, no. 1 (Winter 1992): 101–46, esp. 137–40. For analysis of the role of epistemic communities on the Soviet-American relationship, see Sarah Mendelson, 'Internal Battles and External Wars: Politics, Learning, and the Soviet Withdrawal from Afghanistan,' *World Politics* 45, no. 3 (April 1993): 327–60; and *Changing*

Course: *Ideas, Politics, and the Soviet Withdrawal from Afghanistan* (Princeton: Princeton University Press, 1998), esp. 10; Jeffrey T. Checkel, 'Ideas, Institutions, and the Gorbachev Foreign Policy Revolution,' *World Politics* 45, no. 2 (Jan. 1993): 242–70; and *Ideas and International Political Change: Soviet-Russian Behavior and the End of the Cold War* (New Haven: Yale University Press, 1997); Thomas Risse-Kappen, 'Ideas Do Not Float Freely: Transnational Coalitions, Domestic Structures, and the End of the Cold War,' *International Organization* 48, no. 2 (Spring 1994): 185–214; and Robert Herman, 'Identity, Norms, and National Security: The Soviet Foreign Policy Revolution and the End of the Cold War,' in *The Culture of National Security: Norms and Identity in World Politics*, ed. Peter J. Katzenstein (New York: Columbia University Press, 1996), 271–316.

31 On the multiple roles of Southern researchers, see Richard Stren, 'Urban Research and Urban Researchers in Developing Countries' *International Social Science Journal* 48, no. 1 (March 1996): 107–19.

32 For an excellent discussion of the concept of policy communities as applied to Canada, see Evert Lindquist, 'Public Managers and Policy Communities: Learning to Meet New Challenges,' *Canadian Public Administration* 35, no. 2 (Summer 1991): 127–59. For a more general analysis of the historical development of the concepts of both policy network and policy community, the reader is referred to Michael M. Atkinson and William D. Coleman, 'Policy Networks, Policy Communities, and the Problems of Governance,' in *Policy Studies in Canada: The State of the Art*, ed. Laurent Dobuzinskis, Michael Howlett, and David Laycock (Toronto: University of Toronto Press, 1996), 193–218.

33 On the 'bureaucratic' and 'post-bureaucratic' models of organization, see Michael Barzelay, *Breaking through Bureaucracy* (Berkeley: University of California Press, 1992).

34 Hugh Heclo, 'Issue Networks and the Executive Establishment,' in *The New American Political System*, ed. Anthony King (Washington, DC: American Enterprise Institute for Public Policy Research, 1978), 87–124.

35 Budd L. Hall, 'Looking Back, Looking Forward: Reflections on the Origins of the International Participatory Research Network and the Participatory Research Group in Toronto, Canada' (unpublished paper prepared for the 8th World Congress on Participatory Action Research, Cartegena, Colombia, n.d.), 10.

36 Chris Argyris and Donald A. Schon, *Organizational Learning: A Theory of Action Perspective* (Boston: Addison-Wesley, 1978); Donald Schon, *The Reflective Practitioner: How Professionals Think in Action* (New York: Basic Books, 1983); Chris Argyris and Donald Schon, *Strategy, Change and Defensive*

Routines (Boston: Pitman, 1985); and David Bohm, ed., *Thought as a System* (London: Routledge, 1994).

37 Peter Senge, *The Fifth Discipline: The Art and Practice of the Learning Organization* (New York: Doubleday, 1991). The 'five disciplines' proposed by Senge are systems thinking, personal mastery, the development of mental models, the articulation of a shared vision, and team learning. For an excellent collection of related writings by other authors and practitioners, see Sarita Chawla and John Renesch, eds, *Learning Organizations: Developing Cultures for Tomorrow's Workplace* (Portland: Productivity Press, 1995).

38 In the literature on the learning organization, there is an intimate relationship between research and theory building. Good managers should be involved in both. The following advice is offered in an article by the co-founder of the MIT Organizational Learning Center: 'Managers need to become theory-builders within their own organizations. They must create new frameworks within which they continually test their strategies, policies, and decisions to inform them of improvements on the organization's design. It is no longer sufficient to apply generic theories and frameworks like band-aids to one's own specific issues. Managers must take the best of the new ideas and build a workable theory for their own organization. As theory-builders, managers must have an intimate knowledge of how their organization works as a whole' (Daniel H. Kim, 'Managerial Practice Fields: Infrastructures of a Learning Organization,' in Chawla and Renesch, eds, *Learning Organizations*, 362.

39 Senge, *Fifth Discipline*, 287.

40 See Gibbons et al., *New Production of Knowledge*, 28–43.

41 Lisa Peattie, 'Urban Research in the 1990s,' in *Preparing for the Urban Future: Global Pressures and Local Forces*, ed. Michael A. Cohen, Blair Ruble, Joseph Tulchin, and Allison Garland (Washington, DC: Woodrow Wilson Center Press, 1996), 371–91. Peattie begins by recapitulating Aristotle's distinction between three kinds of knowledge: universal knowledge (the ideal of pure science – knowledge that is eternal and can be demonstrated to be true), technique ('the art or craft of bringing something into being'), and *phronesis* (often translated as 'prudence,' or 'knowledge of what to do in particular circumstances'). In many respects, these forms of knowledge parallel traditional science and social science, engineering science, and policy science respectively. But *phronesis*, which touches on what is conventionally labelled as 'operational knowledge,' combines the first two: general principles derived from rigorous comparative study and practical technique. For Peattie, an ideal way to obtain *phronesis* is the case study method.

42 Bent Flyvbjerg, *Rationality and Power: Democracy in Practice* (Chicago: University of Chicago Press, 1998).

43 David Swartz, *Culture and Power: The Sociology of Pierre Bourdieu* (Chicago: University of Chicago Press, 1997), 50.

44 Pierre Bourdieu, *Distinction*, trans. Richard Nice (London: Routledge and Kegan Paul, 1984).

CHAPTER TWO

Knowledge Production and Global Civil Society

Janice Gross Stein

Knowledge Networks in Global Civil Society

We are interested in knowledge networks in part because of what they tell us about new forms of global organization and communication in the wake of the revolution in information technology. Fluid, horizontal networks are a different type of structure from either hierarchically organized states or global markets. As information technology multiplies the possibility of networks of exchange, it is important to understand how networks work in the shadow of states. Evaluation of the five knowledge networks examined in this volume should suggest at least the broad outlines of possible relationships among networks and hierarchies. How autonomous are networks from states and international institutions? Do they stand freely, or are they grafted onto national or international institutions in ways that are not yet clearly understood? The answers to these questions can help us to begin the mapping of knowledge networks in the shadow of national and international institutions.

Knowledge networks may matter for another reason. Much is currently being written about the decline of the state as an autonomous actor in international politics in the face of global markets and the growth of international civil society, world civic politics, and transnational advocacy networks.[1] The 'new diplomacy,' a network of NGOs and like-minded states is credited, for example, with achieving the ban on anti-personnel landmines. There is no consensus, however, on what these concepts mean.[2] Nor do analysts of global civil society distinguish clearly between knowledge networks and other forms of associational activity in global political space.

Domestic civic society developed historically alongside states that exercised authority and power, and often a monopoly of force. Associations grew around the state, initially drawing political and economic support from the 'private,' rather than the public, sector. There is no international analogue to a 'strong' state that has a monopoly of force and stands apart from global civil society. Nor are the 'private' economic and political roots of a global civil society obvious or unproblematic.

The Secretary-General of the United Nations does not differentiate clearly between global and local civil society. In introducing his program for reform of the United Nations, Kofi Annan observed: 'Overall, civil society's increasing influence is contributing to a process of enlargement of international cooperation and spurring the United Nations system and other intergovernmental structures toward greater transparency and accountability and closer linkages between national and international levels of decision-making and implementing.'[3] NGOs and other civil society actors are perceived not only as disseminators of information or providers of services but also as shapers of global policy. The Secretary-General promised that every department in the United Nations would designate a liaison officer 'to facilitate access by [global] civil society to the U.N. At the country level ... the U.N. system should create more opportunities for tripartite cooperation with governments and civil society.'[4]

Some analysts of transnational groups suggest that these networks of activists are more than policy networks that lobby national and international institutions. They are 'political actors in their own right,' because they use 'diverse mechanisms of governance to alter and shape widespread behavior.'[5] The target of network activity is broadly defined: governments, international institutions, multinational corporations, and citizens. These networks act across the increasingly porous boundaries between states and civil societies. Through their actions, they build capacity within society and inadvertently contribute to the creation of a global civil society by influencing values and behaviour across societies.

There is evidence of growing texture to 'global' civil society, or civil society that extends beyond the boundaries of a single state. The Union of International Associations lists more than fifteen thousand NGOs that operate in three or more countries and that draw their finances from sources in more than one country. In 1948, forty-one NGOs had consultative status at the United Nations; by 1997, more than twelve hundred had been granted such status. Internationally active NGOs, using current communication and information technologies, are connecting in worldwide networks that reach around their governments. These networks of NGOs connect local civil societies to global spaces even as local NGOs provide the critical supports for global activity.

At a minimum, global civil society can refer to private exchanges across state borders. Such a broad definition, however, would encompass the vast array of exchange and transactional relationships of the global private sector driven by profit maximization, and would not capture the normative content of domestic 'civic society,' which includes associational linkages and commitment to civic virtues. We use 'global civil society' to designate that private space beyond state borders that extends beyond economic exchange yet is not governed explicitly by international institutions. This space encompasses the associations and networks that are committed to 'civic' or participatory values. Global civil society does not include the vast range of private corporations and associations that are active for private gain, but rather the associations and NGOs that are engaged in the development of global public policy for the 'public good.'

The emphasis on transnational network activity draws heavily on analyses of the significant role of associational networks in the creation of domestic civil society. Analyses of 'social capital' suggest that dense networks of association within societies play a significant role in both democracy and development as well as in the creation of a vibrant civil society.[6] The importance of associations and networks has been extended to global society, where their impact is differentiated along several dimensions. Working within the pluralist tradition, some analysts conceive of advocacy networks as lobbying through the increasingly porous border between state and society for democratization and civil society in those states where it currently does not exist.[7] Here, networks work from the global to the local. Networks also work 'up' from the local to the global; they lobby international institutions on issues of global public policy.[8] Others see networks as promoters of new international norms that in turn reinforce international institutions. This last role of advocacy networks is consistent with the role of knowledge networks, which generate new knowledge, often, though not always, with the purpose of informing policy development and implementation.

Some observers are more sceptical of the role of networks in civil society. They worry that some of the global associational activity can erode the power of elected institutions and vest it in international institutions and multinational corporations that are not accountable to any broadly based electorate. These processes contribute to a 'democratic deficit,' as the state 'shrinks,' is 'hollowed out,' or fragments.[9] Even the global activities of NGOs, many of whom are explicitly committed to democratic norms, can at times be troubling. Inequities of power and access to resources can lead to the weakening of NGOs in poorer societies when stronger partners with richer resources take the lead. The fluidity of transnational networks, precisely the attribute that facilitates adaptation and innovation, can also endanger vulnerable members who are left behind – and exposed – as networks dissolve.[10]

These two strands of argument about the role of non-governmental networks are too broad to be evaluated against the particular experience of the knowledge networks. Knowledge networks should be more limited in their impact on an emergent global civil society than transnational advocacy networks. When the social context of knowledge generation and the expanded concept of knowledge production characteristic of networks that connect North and South are taken into consideration, however, the impact of knowledge networks on local and global civil society may be considerable.

We consider the production of knowledge as a social process. The collection of knowledge, its production, and processes of dissemination are all shaped by the social context in which these processes take place. Knowledge networks, located in communities, may be better able to access and bring to the forefront the local knowledge which is often so important in defining a problem and shaping the agenda. Knowledge networks also contribute to capacity building, empower local experts independently of government, and create social centres of expertise. To the extent that knowledge networks engage broadly with the policy implications of the knowledge they generate, they may also strengthen local networks of policy experts and, through these networks, make a contribution to local civic society. Indeed, we argue that the formal separation between 'academic' and 'policy' knowledge becomes blurred in global knowledge networks.

Examination of these five knowledge networks can shed light on the capacity of networks to strengthen members in their own civil – or not so civil – societies, to connect members across borders so that they can organize politically in the public space outside international institutions, and to promote norms of participation in public policy-making at the national and international levels.[11] Evaluation of these networks can help assess whether these kinds of contributions are at all likely, or appropriate, even as it provides a glimpse of an increasingly networked world.

The Quality of Knowledge in Knowledge Networks

Any assessment of the impact of knowledge networks on global civil society depends significantly on an evaluation of the quality and kinds of knowledge they produce. We are interested in whether these networks generate innovative research agendas, produce significant research, and disseminate knowledge effectively and quickly. These are traditional criteria for the evaluation of knowledge, broadly acceptable across fields of expertise and across cultures. These traditional criteria do not permit a complete assessment of the emergent role of knowledge networks in a nascent global civil society. Here, we will need additional criteria.

It is difficult even to use traditional criteria to evaluate the contribution of these knowledge networks. Their particular expertise requires evaluation from within the appropriate research communities. Surprisingly, the sponsoring foundations and donors have not undertaken this kind of systematic assessment, nor, by and large, have the networks themselves.[12] As a result, much of the data that are required for a systematic evaluation are not available.

Even if better data were available, a valid set of generic measures is not obvious, especially since the appropriate reference group is both unclear and potentially infinite. It is not clear because we could compare these knowledge networks to each other, to independent research institutes organized in more traditional ways, or to the knowledge that each of the network members may have created as an individual scholar and scientist. As an initial attempt at assessment, we ask three counterfactual questions of each network:

- Would we know *less* if this network had not been created? Did the network push the research agenda in a previously unexplored direction?
- Would we know *differently* if network members had not had the opportunity to work together? Did the collaborative effort produce research that would not likely have resulted from individual effort?
- Would we have known what we now know *more slowly* or *less widely* if the network had not disseminated the knowledge it generated? Did the network build capacity in the research community? Did the network build a shared

language across different perspectives? Did the network meet its mandate and operational objectives? Was the network able to disseminate the knowledge it created effectively? Were its processes of knowledge dissemination different from those of established hierarchically organized knowledge centres?

To answer these questions, we do not need to make qualitative judgments about the research that was produced. We do assess the process through which knowledge was produced and transferred.

There is an additional set of criteria that relates more closely to knowledge networks that seek to inform and influence global public policy issues. Global public policy networks link together researchers across sectors of society to draw on information and knowledge from different sources.[13] They often seek to use the knowledge they create and disseminate to put new issues on the global public policy agenda or give prominence to issues that are not receiving attention. Indeed, as we shall argue, academic and policy knowledge are synergistic in global knowledge networks in ways that are quite distinct from the work of individual researchers. To assess their impact on global public policy development, it is useful to consider:

- *the sustainability of knowledge that is created;*
  Of interest is not only the capacity to continue the research begun by the network, but also the life of the ideas in public discussion within the broader community. Did network researchers inject ideas into policy discussions, and did these ideas find their way into policy documents?
- *the platforms for knowledge creation;*
  Network researchers are at times able to open channels of communication and collaborative research that otherwise would not have existed. In so doing, they create platforms for continuing policy work that can spin off from the main network.
- *the recruitment and training of young knowledge creators;*
  Networks at times deliberately set out to engage and connect young members who would otherwise not have access to policy ideas and policy discussion.

The judgments we make on all these criteria are tentative, and relative to real and imagined alternatives. With these qualifications, the evidence from the five networks does suggest significant contributions by most of these networks on some of these measures.[14]

Evaluating Knowledge Networks

The record of GURI provides the clearest positive answer to most of these questions. Its mandate was broad: to produce research that enhances understanding of urban issues in the South and to help to inform policies on urban issues. The network produced a comprehensive analysis of existing urban research, tapped sources of knowledge among the partners that were not previously widely known, identified important gaps in knowledge, and shaped an innovative research program on urban governance that reflected the diverse concerns of its members. There is a considerable record of publication, all of it comparative, and none the likely output of a single scholar or institute. The network's contribution to urban studies was recognized when it was accredited as a participant in the preparatory process and the official meeting of Habitat II, the global conference on cities held in Istanbul in June 1996. GURI succeeded in pushing the frontiers of knowledge about urban governance in Asia, Africa, and Latin America.

Interestingly, network members themselves did not give great weight to the considerable published materials. They emphasized rather the kind of knowledge that has been produced and its dissemination within local communities. As one member explained:

> The knowledge that we are constructing is practical because it has been formed through the experiences of real actors who determine the possibility of urban governance. This knowledge, or these knowledges, is neither purely technical nor purely theoretical. Rather, it is the fruit of interaction between researchers, politicians, and community leaders that have set themselves the task of analysing how relations between civil society and local governments are created, to achieve better management of the city and also to contribute to the historical construction of the citizenry in such a way that the people of the communities can participate fully in the creation of their own cities, where they live.[15]

This mode of knowledge production is qualitatively different from the kind of research that academics conventionally do, and reflected the movement by researchers, working with colleagues in NGOs, multiple levels of government, and the private sector, into a more problem-oriented, transdisciplinary direction. The third phase of the network extended this approach even further.[16] If GURI members had not had the opportunity to work together, both across regions and within communities, it is difficult to imagine how this comparative knowledge of urban governance, informed by theoretical issues and practical concerns, would have been created. It is clear that we do know *differently* as a result of the network.

The modalities of the research made dissemination to local communities relatively easy. Insofar as local community leaders, NGOs, and government officials, both elected and appointed, worked with GURI members on operational problems of governance, in some communities dissemination occurred through the process of building problem-oriented knowledge. In knowledge networks generically, processes of knowledge creation and dissemination are not separated into phased sequences, but interact dynamically as dissemination by local participants generates feedback and refines local knowledge, which in turn reshapes more generic knowledge. The evidence suggests that we know *more widely* as a result of GURI activities.

There is strong evidence as well that GURI developed capacity and strengthened the support available to researchers in the regions. GURI actively sought young researchers and gave them the opportunity to meet and work with senior researchers from around the globe. For the members of the network, GURI has provided an unprecedented opportunity for exchange and learning across geographic regions and academic disciplines. It has also provided researchers in Africa, Asia, the Middle East, and Latin America with financial resources, publishing opportunities, professional contacts, and access to both international agencies and local policy-makers. Researchers were able to organize meetings that brought in top specialists, officials, and donor agency representatives; they might not otherwise have had access to as diverse a group of experts, funders, and officials. GURI provided, for many of its members, a window on the international research and policy scene.

We suggested earlier that networks may empower members in their own societies by enhancing their status and their access to resources. Several members gave special emphasis to GURI's importance in increasing their access to resources when adverse political or financial conditions were limiting the opportunities for research in their own countries.[17] In some cases, network membership translated into greater visibility and influence, facilitating entry into other networks and academic and policy-making circles.

CISEPO also has scientific and policy objectives, but, unlike GURI, the two sets of objectives are not intrinsically related. CISEPO seeks to exchange medical knowledge and, in the process, to contribute to peace-building among parties in conflict with one another. It is even more difficult to evaluate a contribution to peace-building than it is to assess a contribution to scientific knowledge; success in peace-building is often the product of long lead times and multiple factors which interact in complex and poorly understood ways. We rely heavily, as does the network, on the subjective assessments of the process by the partners in the projects where peace-building is an objective.

CISEPO runs a Fellowships for Peace Program. More than twenty physicians and scientists from Australia, Brazil, China, Hungary, Ireland, Israel, the Netherlands, New Zealand, Poland, and Turkey have visited as fellows and academics to study, conduct research, develop their knowledge base, and participate in departmental, hospital, university, and scientific projects. They then returned to their countries to transfer knowledge and technology, contribute to the professional development of their colleagues, and initiate cross-disciplinary interactions within their medical communities. Many of these physicians and scientists now occupy senior academic and service positions, several with professorial appointments. Many participants in CISEPO's exchange programs continue to participate in network-related activities following their stay in the host country through ongoing contributions to CISEPO's research, clinical, and volunteer health service programs. CISEPO members have published articles regularly in scientific journals and lecture in public forums under the auspices of CISEPO, and joint collaborative research projects that emerge from CISEPO's programs have resulted in a range of publications.[18]

CISEPO also operates joint educational and clinical programs that include research prizes, continuing education programs, international scientific meetings, and elective programs for undergraduate students. The continuing medical education program conducts a series of educational events in Canada and in the Middle East which promote basic and applied research, clinical guidelines and protocols, training, disease management, and epidemiological studies.

In part as a result of continuing education workshops held in the Middle East, CISEPO is increasingly designing collaborative projects with the parties to a conflict. CISEPO and the governments of Jordan and Israel launched a trilateral otolaryngology collaborative project in 1996. A year later, CISEPO and the governments of Israel, Jordan, and the Palestinian Authority launched a project to address hearing loss in children. This initiative on child hearing loss was developed in response to invitations from the Ministers of Health in Israel and the Palestinian Authority and the Director of the Royal Jordanian Medical Services. This workshop significantly restructured and expanded the scope of CISEPO's continuing education program. The program now includes a travelling faculty of representatives from each country who have collaborated on a series of four seminars in the Middle East. Three of the workshops addressed hearing loss, and one, surgical skills. There are plans to initiate continuing education programs in other areas of medical specialization.

The scientific contribution of these programs has been evaluated through procedures routinely embedded in the process of clinical research and medical treatment. Established in 1994, the Molecular Biology Laboratory and Cancer Research Program at Tel Aviv University and the Rabin Medical Centre is the result of a shared vision with CISEPO. It is now the leading thyroid and larynx cancer centre in the region. Very few clinical departments in the region have research facilities closely connected to them, but this project links the conceptual and the operational, the laboratory and the clinic, in order to advance research and dissemination while delivering medical services. The head of the program, Dr Raphael Feinmesser, and his staff won a Government of Israel Award for their research on cancer of the larynx.[19] He was 'very doubtful' that this project would have begun without CISEPO.

Measuring success in peace-building is more difficult; the criteria need to be modest and long-term. Within the network, a program is considered a successful peace-building project if knowledge is enhanced or transmitted, and if the parties complete the project with the intention and desire to collaborate further on a professional or personal level. There is evidence that some of CISEPO's partners wish to continue their collaboration.

The collaborative conferences cultivate and sustain personal relationships as well as the exchange of knowledge among Israeli, Jordanian, and Egyptian physicians. Dr Feinmesser in Israel now has direct and ongoing contact between his counterparts in these countries over shared issues of scientific concern. If CISEPO had not initiated and facilitated these activities, he concluded, 'this would not have happened.'[20] CISEPO made possible the first step, which allowed physicians in Israel to work directly with their colleagues in Jordan and Egypt without going through the coordinator of the network. One network has spun off another.

The head of the program in Jordan, Dr Mohammed Al Masri, is also pleased with the project performance thus far. It is possible that the hearing-loss project might have been implemented, though not in collaboration with the Israeli physicians, without CISEPO's efforts, because it was so desperately needed in Jordan. He maintains, however, that the peace-building component would certainly not have occurred without CISEPO; Al Masri would not have contacted his counterparts in Israel. Now he is in regular contact with Feinmesser and his colleagues from Tel Aviv. He also now works with Arab Israelis and communicates with the coordinator of CISEPO regularly via e-mail and by phone. The doctors have established positive working relationships and have developed a mutual respect on both professional and personal levels. Al Masri now wants to take this process one step further, by establishing a research organization and a related clinic in collaboration with CISEPO as an example of tangible benefits from cooperation between Jordanians and Israelis.

The analysis suggests that in specific areas of medical science, such as the diagnostics of child hearing loss and treatment of cancer of the nasopharynx, CISEPO has been successful in advancing knowledge through collaborative research. The network is far stronger, however, in transferring and disseminating clinical knowledge through its partnership programs. It seems fair to conclude that as a consequence of this network, *clinical knowledge* has improved.

An even stronger claim can be made that CISEPO has brought together respected scientists who, because of political conflict and cultural difference, would not otherwise have collaborated. The clinical programs that were developed would certainly not have been put in place without the network. CISEPO's success in building collaborative partnerships across political divides accelerates the process of knowledge transfer. These partnerships built capacity, provided training opportunities for young physicians, created opportunities to share clinical information, and enhanced research and clinical partnerships. CISEPO's strength is its capacity to transfer knowledge and improve clinical practice across barriers that would otherwise stand as obstacles and, in the process, create platforms for expanded collaborative research and new networks.

CARNET made a major contribution to knowledge of the social implications of an aging population. Of the five networks, its productivity was the most impressive: it produced research in four major areas that led to 177 peer-reviewed articles, 85 chapters in books,

9 complete books, and 483 invited papers and lectures provided by CARNET researchers. One group focused on the need for products and services that would enhance independence later in life; a second, on the prevalence and impact of employees' involvement in work and family (particularly eldercare) responsibilities; a third, on how cognitive ability changes across the adult years and how these changes affect the performance of older adults at work and in their daily lives; and a fourth sought to explore the complex demographic dynamics of the Canadian labour force and to identify existing and planned human resource practices and policies that affect the changing age structure of the workplace. Overall, the research groups focused on the changing individual, work and family contexts, and the identification and provision of products and services to meet various needs over life courses and in later years. We know far more as a result of the research conducted through CARNET.

CARNET was also successful at producing operational knowledge from conceptual research. Dr Fergus Craik, who directed the Cognitive Function Research Group, considered that the network projects 'pushed the lab closer to the real world.'[21] Through the network, he developed constructive partnerships with hospitals and other organizations, and new projects developed. Researchers partnered, for example, with the Alberta Motor League and a local hospital to examine aging and driving capacity, and the successful partnership continues even without the network. This link between conceptual and operational knowledge would not otherwise have happened.

The network helped as well to promote relationships between researchers within their respective fields. The interaction within the cognitive group, across universities, was very positive and clearly facilitated by the network. CARNET also brought together groups within psychology who were engaged in similar research and who otherwise would not have worked together. From the perspective of the head of the cognitive group, there unquestionably was 'value added.' CARNET made possible meaningful interaction within disciplines and effectively linked operational and conceptual knowledge. Finally, as a result of the broad network of partnerships, research results were disseminated quickly and widely. We can conclude with confidence that not only do we know *more*, but we also know *differently* and *more widely* as a result of the network.

CoRR encourages and facilitates interdisciplinary approaches and practices for coastal resource development and management. The principal contribution of the network appears to lie not so much in generating new biological research on mollusc culture, but rather in reframing the research problems so that biological knowledge is situated within the larger social, economic, and political context of community life. The central focus is the sustainable livelihoods of coastal communities and community-based coastal resource management. Here, the social processes of knowledge production and generation are clear. Through CoRR, we know *differently* and more *widely.*

CoRR's newsletter, *Out of the Shell*, provides a forum for researchers to analyse studies on mollusc culturing and to exchange results. It contains short reports, longer articles – sometimes in the form of research papers – by project scientists, articles written by the coordinator on mollusc culture research and commercial development, comprehensive bibliographies, Internet source information, details from conferences, and forums for readers to dialogue.

The central coordinating office screens for the needs of communities for mollusc culture technology, provides literature searches for individuals in developing countries who are working on mollusc culture, and suggests new ideas for research. Researchers also regularly exchange reports of technical progress, research problems, and other aspects of mollusc culture. The network holds workshops and working-group meetings, and in 1997 began a summer institute to promote and facilitate direct exchanges between researchers. Network members also regularly share their research at non-network conferences. CoRR holds network meetings roughly once a year, as well as the annual summer institute. These research and workshop presentations have generated publications in partnership with universities and institutes in the South.[22]

The network has also helped to build capacity. CoRR works with students at universities who have scholarships through projects that IDRC, its funder, supports, and many of these projects explicitly involve graduate students or recently completed doctorates in the research. The network has also worked with researchers in developing countries who collaborate actively with local NGOs to engage communities in resource management and planning within the context of socio-economic needs. CoRR supports these researchers as they assist communities to address obstacles to resource conservation and management. CoRR also actively works with regional organizations to complement their expertise and contacts and to advance their research agenda. As a result, the conceptual is related to the operational. The research questions of CoRR members are frequently pragmatic, and their findings are communicated proactively to community members as CoRR project members assist in training community leaders and enhancing local knowledge. The reverse is also true: by partnering with local organizations, CoRR project members benefit from their knowledge and experience, and feed back local knowledge into the project.

CoRR's success encouraged the organization of a spin-off network to reinforce and deepen the research collaboration. The new network, Island Sustainability, Livelihood, and Equity (ISLE), links four universities in Canada with universities in the island nations of Indonesia and the Philippines, and in the Caribbean. Its research is interdisciplinary: ISLE seeks to strengthen island partner institutions responsible for human resource development and to promote the effective translation of this knowledge and institutional development into action-oriented policies and into programs designed to ensure sustainable island development. It explicitly seeks to feed back the knowledge it generates into the goals, objectives, programs, and policies of sustainable development in Canada in general, and specifically in Canada's island and coastal regions.

The most significant accomplishment of CoRR is its broadening, indeed reshaping, of the research agenda, both within CoRR and in the spin-off network. This expanded research agenda very much reflects the perspective of the director of the network that scientific development 'cannot be done in isolation from the real world where scientific knowledge is needed.' He acknowledges that 'systems interact, not only biological and physical systems but these and the social and economic systems.' As a result, he suggests that 'our precious technology may not be relevant in a complex world unless the users can profit by it and not compromise traditional and essential livelihood sources. The problem of non-utilization of technology is often not the technology but the lack of fit to the user's lifestyle and economic situation.'[23] The reshaping of the research agenda, the multidisciplinary focus, and the prominent involvement of partners to capture local knowledge make it very likely that not only do we know differently as a result of CoRR, we know far more widely.

LEAP's effectiveness is more difficult to assess, in part because of the breadth of its mandate, in part because its mandate is less research than it is community development, education, and policy activism at both regional and international levels, and in part because it works with the environmental and adult education communities, who had previously not worked together. LEAP sees its mandate as bringing adult education to the fore within the environmental community and bringing environmental issues to the attention of the adult education community. Although the network has initiated and facilitated research to achieve these objectives, its principal efforts have been to lobby and to disseminate knowledge from one community to another.[24]

LEAP has lobbied actively to bring to the attention of each community the knowledge developed by the other. LEAP members worked successfully for changes to Agenda 21 at the international conference on the environment in Rio de Janeiro in 1992. At the UNESCO Fifth International Conference on Adult Education, held in Hamburg in 1997, it was one of two lead agencies for the environmental adult education thematic group. As a result of coordinated activity, environmental issues were for the first time included on the agenda of a major international adult education meeting.

LEAP has also worked to transfer knowledge across communities. In conjunction with community groups, LEAP is involved in the development of a training manual on facilitating environmental adult education. It has convened meetings in the South to promote environmental adult education: in Fiji, for example, through the 'Saving the Plants That Save Lives' project, LEAP brought together women from around the world to discuss traditional medicine and adult education; and in Kenya, where women began to burn plastic because they had run out of fuelwood, LEAP provided materials on the hazards of burning plastic and organized a number of workshops for women to discuss the problem and develop solutions. In Uganda, LEAP has trained environmental adult education trainers.

Conclusion

We cannot draw wide-ranging conclusions from this analysis of five networks. Our examination of these cases, which span a considerable range of research foci and organizational styles, nevertheless does suggest that networks of this kind are making a particular kind of contribution to knowledge, a contribution that in part reflects their wide, horizontal structures, and in part the recognition by the leaders of several of these networks of the importance of the social context in which knowledge is generated. Knowledge networks, drawing on local resources, also contribute to an emergent global civil society. These knowledge networks brought three special advantages.

The networks were able to generate new knowledge in large part because partners brought knowledge to the table that would otherwise have been missed. Whether it is the 'local' knowledge embedded in coastal communities, or the knowledge of urban governance in the Caribbean that scientists from the region brought to the definition of a global project, this knowledge played an important part in defining research priorities and in shaping research agendas. Some of these networks were also successful in seeding capacity and in expanding the possibilities for future partnerships.

These networks also paid explicit attention to 'operational' knowledge, or the interaction between the knowledge of research centres and academic institutions, and that embedded within communities. The development of operational knowledge is far more than a straightforward process of translation of generic knowledge into language that is understandable and useful to communities. It is also the process of drawing upon, and transmitting, knowledge from communities that is critical to the formulation of the research problem and the research questions, and the design of iterative processes so that interaction among the different knowledge communities continues. The emphasis on operational knowledge was central, for example, to the research on sustainable coastal communities, on adult environmental education, and in the last phase of GURI's work on urban governance. This kind of knowledge, important and valuable, is often overlooked in more formal research settings. We call this process 'the social generation of knowledge.'

Knowledge that is socially generated through a global network is likely to be informed by, and responsive to, policy questions. In GURI, for example, researchers from the South put urgent policy questions on the agenda, questions that shaped the global research agenda to a significant extent. Policy questions were not a supplement to the principal research agenda, but central to the concerns of a diverse community of researchers. The challenge of disseminating knowledge then takes on a somewhat different cast when members of a global network, who have participated in defining the research and shaping the agenda, are also the principal disseminators. Often respected in their local communities, their stature at times enhanced by their participation in the network, members can transmit ideas or results in ways that are more connected and, therefore, likely more effective than more formal strategies of dissemination that speak to, rather than from within, communities. Members are also likely to engage in local civil society, to the extent that conditions permit, and to communicate their shared knowledge globally as part of the network.

The knowledge networks we analyse in this volume demanded special skills from their leaders, far beyond their formal responsibilities in the academy. Leaders must 'manage' the network's business, 'steer' the development of the network, and coordinate its activities. The business of the network must get done: meetings organized, research monitored, and funding secured. All five networks required 'management' at critical stages in the process of knowledge production. These kinds of tasks are traditionally performed by 'senior' leadership in vertically structured organizations.

Network leaders must also lead. Working within horizontal structures, they must build an effective team and invite members to participate collaboratively in setting the goals, defining the agenda, and structuring research problems. The kinds of skills required to build a collaborative team across cultural divides – sensitivity to differences, respect for different traditions, recognition of differing priorities, and openness to different work patterns – are quite distinct from the management of a centralized command-and-control organization. If leaders do not respect and enhance the flexibility of networks, promote autonomy by members, and encourage and support initiative at all levels, they sacrifice the most important assets that networks provide. Good network leaders are expert conveners, who create opportunities for members to come together to contribute their specialized expertise, which, cumulatively, creates new kinds of knowledge.[25]

It can be misleading, however, to emphasize the uniqueness of global knowledge networks. They require funding and support, as do hierarchically organized research institutes and universities. Networks are not a 'cheap' generator of knowledge; none of these five was self-sustaining, and all required significant and sustained investments from funders. We return to the issue of the special requirements of funders in chapter 8.

These five networks also clung like barnacles to established institutions, primarily universities, relying on their infrastructure, support, and personnel, which they borrowed at low, sometimes no, cost. These five knowledge networks are not alternatives to established research institutions, but complements to them. Without the support of established universities, institutes, and important funders, these networks could not have been created, much less have accomplished what they did. At the same time, the knowledge networks enhance the reach of universities and research institutes as they bring their new and, more to the point, their different knowledge to the table.

If this symbiosis between newer networks and older institutions is a metaphor for the evolving global system, it suggests that the relationship among global networks, states, international institutions, and local and global civil societies is more complex than either proponents or detractors of networks suggest. Networks are participants in local civil societies, but they also need states and institutions, both as supports and as the strategic arm for the operational knowledge they produce. Here, networks look to states. They connect globally to work with international institutions as partners, but, in so doing, they thicken an emergent, fragile, and still partial global civil society. They are grafted onto national or international institutions, but form a web of connections that these institutions themselves do not have. Future research should explore the consequences of the 'thickening' by networks of the web of connections among institutions, locally and globally.

If evidence from these five cases is any guide, knowledge networks can go around, through, under, and over states to reach scientists and scholars, communities, local institutes and universities, regional governments, and international institutions. Evidence drawn from the network on urban governance suggests, for example, that individuals gained status in their own communities as a consequence of their membership in the network. In this sense, they were empowered by the network. Partly as a result of this increased status, members also gained better access to their own governments and, in some but not all cases, were able to press effectively for increased consultation and a more transparent process of policy-making on urban issues.[26] We found no evidence, moreover, that members were disempowered by their participation in the network, that their prior associations were weakened through their participation in a global network, or that the 'global agenda' subsumed the local agenda. On the contrary, the local agenda infused and shaped the global agenda. This pattern may be the result of the extraordinary sensitivity of the leaders in all these networks to the importance of broad-based participation and consensual decision-making, and to the social process of knowledge generation.

It is too early to determine, at least in these five cases, what happens to members when a network dissolves and their access to global resources diminishes. It may be that capacity has been built and their enhanced status allows them to continue to access new resources as well as to participate more effectively in policy-making. On the other hand, with diminished access to the connections and the resources they once had, it is also plausible that members could be more vulnerable to governments determined to monopolize policy-making and power. We need to trace the career trajectories of members after networks' dissolution to evaluate the impact of networks on the strengthening of civil society in their home societies. Likely the impact will be variable, dependent as much on the attributes of societies as on the characteristics of networks.

Finally, we do see evidence of networks using their knowledge to shape the agenda of international institutions. The activity of the network on adult environmental education provides the clearest example. How effective their activity is in comparison to states is presently an unanswerable question. Yet, the recent delay of the multilateral agreement on investment, the treaty banning anti-personnel landmines, and the treaty creating an international criminal court, all suggest that new kinds of relationships may be evolving among networks and states. These kinds of relationships need systematic analysis if we are to understand better how knowledge moves across borders; how, through networks, it bubbles up, out, in and around, above and beneath states; and how knowledge networks contribute to a nascent global civic society.

NOTES

1 Ronnie Lipschutz, 'Reconstructing World Politics: The Emergence of Global Civil Society,' *Millennium* 21, no. 3 (Winter 1992): 389–420; Paul Wapner, 'Politics beyond the State: Environmental Activism and World Civic Politics,' *World Politics* 47 (April 1995): 311–40; Margaret Keck and Kathryn Sikkink, *Activists beyond Borders: Advocacy Networks in International Politics* (Ithaca, NY: Cornell University Press, 1998).

2 James N. Rosenau, *Along the Domestic Foreign Frontier: Exploring Governance in a Turbulent World* (Cambridge: Cambridge University Press, 1997).

3 Kofi Annan, *Program for U.N. Reform* (New York: United Nations, July 1997).

4 Ibid.

5 Wapner, 'Politics beyond the State.' For analysis of policy networks, see Bernd Marin and Renate Mayntz, eds, *Policy Networks: Empirical Evidence and Theoretical Considerations* (Boulder/Frankfurt: Westview/Verlag, 1991).

6 The converging evidence across disciplines and in multiple policy areas is robust. See Robert Putnam, *Making Democracy Work: Civic Traditions in Modern Italy* (Princeton: Princeton University Press, 1993); 'Bowling Alone: America's Declining Social Capital,' *Journal of Democracy* 6, no. 1 (Jan. 1995): 65–78; and 'Tuning In, Tuning Out: The Strange Disappearance of Social Capital in America,' *PS: Political Science and Politics* 28, no. 4 (Dec. 1995): 664–83; Francis Fukuyama, *Trust: The Social Virtues and the Creation of Prosperity* (New York: Free Press, 1995); and James C. Coleman, 'Social Capital in the Creation of Human Capital,' *American Journal of Sociology* (Supplement) 94 (1988): S95–120; and *The Foundations of Social Theory* (Cambridge: Cambridge University Press, 1990).

7 Wapner, 'Politics beyond the State.'

8 Kathryn Sikkink, 'Human Rights, Principled Issue Networks, and Sovereignty in Latin America,' *International Organization* 47, no. 3 (Summer 1993): 411–41.

9 Louis Pauly, 'Capital Mobility, State Autonomy, and Political Legitimacy,' *Journal of International Affairs* 48, no. 2 (Winter 1995): 369–88.

10 See Keck and Sikkink, *Activists beyond Borders*; and Martin Shaw, *Global Society and International Relations* (Cambridge: Polity, 1994).

11 Some of these criteria were explicitly part of the set of expectations of a member of one of the knowledge networks; the network 'could strengthen the visibility of and provide support for people working in NGOs, often in very isolated circumstances, around the world. The network can then contribute to a global civil society, not by appropriating knowledge but rather by strengthening local knowledge and local capacity' (interview, GURI member, network document).

12 One of the networks, CISEPO, does do some evaluation of clinical interventions. The network conducts needs-based assessments and follow-up with patients. Evaluation occurs informally on an ad hoc basis with respect to the peace-building component of the research. Evaluation of continuing education programs is informal, as well. Questionnaires may be used, on occasion, to survey the views of participants.

13 Wolfgang Reinicke and Francis Deng, *Critical Choices: The United Nations, Networks, and the Future of Global Governance* (Ottawa: IDRC, 2000).

14 We experimented with a set of operational measures for each question. Not all measures were relevant to all networks, but when the scores were normalized, GURI and CISEPO ranked first, followed by CARNET and CoRR, and then by LEAP. We do not attach much confidence to these results, partly because of missing data and partly because the validity of these measures has not been tested. At best, they are a crude approximation.

15 Interview, Rafael Emilio Yunen, 21 July 1997.

16 Richard Stren, 'Research on Urban Governance in the Developing World: Toward a New Approach to Comparative Operational Knowledge' (paper presented to the APPAM Conference, Pittsburgh, 1 November 1996).

17 One network member noted, for instance, that the initiative came at a time when local funding for urban research was diminishing, while the research capacity in many developing countries had grown considerably.

18 A recent example includes a CISEPO-supported, multi-hospital-developed document: Philip Cole, Renato Roithmann, Yehudah Roth, and J.S. Chapnik, 'Measures of Airway Patency: A Manual for Users of the Toronto Systems and Others Interested in Nasal Patency Measurement,' *Annals of Otology, Rhinology, and Laryngology* 106, no. 10 (Oct. 1997): 2–5.

19 Dr Feinmesser also benefited professionally from CISEPO. He was at Mount Sinai's ear, nose, and throat (ENT) department on a fellowship when he was appointed Chief of what was to become the Rabin Medical Centre. He needed access to scientific expertise and considered his colleagues in ENT at Mount Sinai to be invaluable. He states that 'the access to expertise and the opportunity to communicate easily and freely at all times with my colleagues at Mount Sinai has been and is crucial in enabling me to do my job.' Feinmesser also appreciates the opportunity to send his residents for education at Mount Sinai and other Toronto teaching hospitals. His residents need both more practice and specialized training (interview, Dr Raphael Feinmesser, 5 September 1997).

20 Interview, Dr Raphael Feinmesser, 5 September 1997.

21 Interview, Dr Fergus Craik, 3 April 1998.

22 CoRR provided partial financial support to the University of the Philippines to publish a collection of case studies on community-based coastal resources management in the Philippines, entitled *Seeds of Hope / Seeds of the Sower*. This collection was a result of the network's Festival Workshop on Community-based Coastal Resources Management. CoRR worked with the University of the Philippines to develop the workshop and to edit the collection. Network researchers also work with related institutes (such as the Marine Science Institute of the University of the Philippines) to publish books. On occasion these books are distributed to member projects and are made available free of charge to interested parties in developing countries. Six books have been published through CoRR support.

23 Interview, Dr Gary Newkirk, *Out of the Shell* 2, no. 2 (1992): 3.

24 LEAP initiated an international research project, Awakening Sleepy Knowledge, in conjunction with the Transformative Learning Centre at OISE, York University's Faculty of Environmental Studies, and CEMINA, a Brazilian

organization that focuses on women, media, and environment issues. The project examined educational dimensions of global environmental action campaigns, particularly those related to food and biodiversity. It resulted in a publication that included comparative regional case studies and conceptual papers. Over five hundred copies were printed and distributed.

25 The qualities of successful network leaders appear to be related to what Daniel Goleman has termed 'emotional intelligence' as well as to traditional measures of intelligence. Goleman's analysis of close to five hundred corporations, government agencies, and NGOs has pointed to the predominant role of emotional, rather than IQ-measured, intelligence in leadership success. Emotional intelligence, which includes self-awareness, the ability to regulate one's emotions, motivation, empathy for others' feelings, and social skills, equips people to operate effectively in networks and in large-scale social organizations in which diversity is a central characteristic. See Daniel Goleman, *Working with Emotional Intelligence* (New York: Bantam Books, 1998).

26 We cannot establish with confidence the impact of the operational knowledge generated by knowledge networks on policy development, largely because no single factor is determining of the complex processes of policy formulation. Analysts of epistemic communities recognize that the impact of consensual scientific knowledge will be a function not only of the effectiveness of the community, but also of the domestic institutions and leaders that shape policy, and of the availability of 'policy windows' for new ideas. See Sarah Mendelson, *Changing Course: Ideas, Politics, and the Soviet Withdrawal from Afghanistan* (Princeton: Princeton University Press, 1998); Thomas Risse-Kappen, 'Ideas Do Not Float Freely:' Transnational Coalitions, Domestic Structure, and the End of the Cold War,' *International Organization* 48, no. 2 (Spring 1994): 185–214; and Janice Gross Stein, 'Political Learning by Doing: Gorbachev as Uncommitted Thinker and Motivated Learner,' *International Organization* 48, no. 2 (Spring 1994): 155–83, esp. 180ff.

CHAPTER THREE

The Canada International Scientific Exchange Program in Otolaryngology

Joy Fitzgibbon

Introduction

Initially conceived as an instrument for bringing scientists and medical practitioners from Israel to Canada for specialized training, the Canada International Scientific Exchange Program in Otolaryngology (CISEPO) gradually expanded its mandate and membership in innovative and challenging directions. CISEPO illustrates the way in which social relationships embedded in a network enable policy entrepreneurs to join seemingly unrelated agendas – in this case, medical research and peacebuilding – and sheds some light on the social foundations of policy change. Specifically, CISEPO shows how personal research partnerships may develop into more extensive and formal institutional relationships between members of different communities and political jurisdictions. It demonstrates how strong personal relationships may sustain a network, particularly in situations of political strain, how these relationships may expand to include other communities, and how an institution founded on purely medical objectives may be transformed to include political ones. CISEPO's experience also reinforces themes that will be evident throughout the five case studies: the importance of creative, diplomatic, and judicious leadership; the strength achieved by rooting network activities in community needs; the necessity of creating administrative structures that effectively evaluate and monitor network outcomes; and the benefits of a generously supported and diversified funding strategy.[1]

Originally called the Isabel Silverman Canada-Israel Scientific Exchange Program in Otolaryngology, CISEPO is a collaborative venture between Mount Sinai Hospital at the University of Toronto and the Saul A. Silverman Family Foundation.[2] Based in the hospital's Department of Otolaryngology, in the first few years of its operation the network conducted an exchange program between the Canadian and Israeli medical communities that focused on research and treatment in otolaryngology. The name was changed in 1986 as institutions from other countries in the Middle East joined the network and as its medical scope expanded to include other sub-specialties. The organization developed gradually without an overarching plan by the network leadership, through the personal contacts of its members.

The character of the network changed in 1995, as the director saw the opportunity to use this scientific collaboration to support the diplomatic peace initiatives then developing between Israel and Jordan. After persistent and patient discussions, CISEPO was invited by the Israeli and Jordanian governments, and later by the newly established Palestinian Authority, to initiate collaborative scientific programs with the explicit goal of bringing together and sustaining links between researchers and practitioners in these countries, who, because of the long-standing political tensions and violence in the region, have traditionally had little or no interaction. CISEPO partners with medical schools in Israel, Jordan, the Palestinian Authority, and China, as well as with those in the more stable environments of Brazil, New Zealand, and the Netherlands. It has established formal agreements with the governments of Jordan and Israel and with the Palestinian Authority. CISEPO incorporated in 1997 as a Canadian charitable organization.

Objectives

CISEPO conducts collaborative medical research, operates a fellowship program to support exchange visits by physicians and surgeons, and designs clinical education programs that enhance scientific knowledge in the treatment of public health problems. By developing partnerships across borders and sparking discussions between disciplines, CISEPO uses the process of knowledge generation to strengthen personal and professional relationships between researchers and practitioners. These interdependent relationships, and the carefully constructed program interventions that emerge from them, are the vehicles through which CISEPO helps to construct the foundations for cooperation and stability in regions characterized by political tensions or violence. As programs operate in environments where civil society is often weak and resources scarce, CISEPO's programs are frequently designed to strengthen local capacities to respond to regional health needs.

Governance

Structure of the Network

Dr Arnold Noyek, Otolaryngologist-in-Chief at Mount Sinai Hospital in Toronto, chairs CISEPO, while a board of directors that includes fellow physicians in the ENT department, medical representatives interested in international health, members of the Silverman Family Foundation, and community representatives governs the network's operations. The board has grown larger over the past few years as the network has expanded its projects; it meets or is consulted approximately every six-to-eight weeks.

CISEPO's projects are directed by physicians based at teaching hospitals in Toronto, their responsibilities divided according to geographical regions and areas of specialization. The project directors construct research groups within these regional projects and work closely with their international partners and with Noyek, who presents project proposals and progress reports to the board members for final approval.

While CISEPO is very much a collaborative venture, the network is dependent upon Noyek's leadership, and he is central to its functioning. As network director, he sits on the board and reports to it, yet he possesses a high degree of freedom to construct, encourage, facilitate, and implement network projects and fund-raising efforts. His leadership style with the board, as with all partners in the network, is to steadily foster positive personal relationships to underpin their collective professional efforts. Consequently, Noyek engenders trust among the leadership team, and this trust has led to a structure that combines embedded accountability on major network initiatives with a high degree of flexibility on the day-to-day operations of the network.

The network has two paid staff members: Noyek's assistant at Mount Sinai juggles responsibilities, operating as administrator of both the network and the department. Noyek's stepbrother, Philip Aber, is the policy and planning adviser, whose major responsibilities are to establish a formal infrastructure to support the integration of policy activities with scientific research and medical treatment. Both staff members report to Noyek and are the only two network members to receive a salary for their CISEPO work.

On an ad hoc and informal basis, Noyek seeks direction from outside advisers. Leo Kramer, for example, is a Washington-based business analyst who examines trade, high-risk multidisciplinary problem-solving, and general business management issues within the Middle East. Kramer advises Noyek on how to establish and develop contacts with Palestinians in the region and has assisted in developing CISEPO's trilateral programs between Israel, Palestine, and Jordan.

Mount Sinai Hospital plays a supportive role, enabling Noyek to use the Department of Otolaryngology as a home for CISEPO; welcoming CISEPO fellows as exchange visitors; strengthening and sustaining the link with international team members by making them, where appropriate and merited, associate staff members of Mount Sinai; allowing the departmental administrator to work on CISEPO business; and providing information on CISEPO activities on the hospital web page. Noyek places CISEPO-related issues on the agenda at departmental meetings and seeks advice on project development from members of the department, the administration of Mount Sinai, and the university's Faculty of Medicine and Program on International Health.

The network's organizational structure is flexible, allowing for fluid relationships. Noyek states that members have the opportunity to strengthen and expand their partnerships and research agendas as authority is delegated, in turn, to the project directors and to the international partners. The structure of governance is horizontal, rather than hierarchical.

Coordination and Decision-Making

Noyek reports to the board, both formally and informally, on the network's progress. CISEPO also provides annual reports to Mount Sinai Hospital. Noyek believes decisions must be made between network members based on consensus, a consequence of the sustained informal collaboration that drives the network. Members of the network also respectfully challenge each other's ideas. As network director, Noyek suggests, 'I have only one vote. Some of my ideas are great; some of my ideas are not. This network must be democratic or it simply will not work.'

Despite the lack of formal structural representation on the board, the individuals with whom we spoke perceive that Noyek is responsive to their concerns and confirm that respectful cooperation is an operational norm. Dr Mohammed Al Masri, Chief of Audiology at King Hussein Medical Centre in Amman, Jordan, describes the process of agenda setting as 'cooperative.' During an interview for this case study, Dr Al Masri introduced an idea for further funding from

CISEPO that he planned to propose to Noyek. Dr Raphael Feinmesser, Chair of Otolaryngology at Rabin Medical Centre in Tel Aviv, Israel, states that he and his staff are able to communicate 'easily and freely at all times' with Noyek and his staff.

As the Toronto office collaborates with those in whom it has personal confidence, Noyek's colleagues operate with relative autonomy. Most are prominent scientists in their respective fields and are unusually broad-minded in their approach. They have, therefore, a high level of respect for each other; however, against this backdrop of mutual respect, they do not hesitate, as Noyek diplomatically suggests, to 'convince by persuasive argument.' For instance, during one of the interviews for this case study, a Toronto partner carefully yet forcefully challenged Noyek in front of the interviewer.

Few formal obligations are attached to membership. According to Noyek, so far they have been 'lucky.' However, the obligations and responsibilities to produce high-quality research programs are embedded in the personal relationships upon which this network is built or, in some cases, which this network has fostered. CISEPO chooses network members carefully, considering more than their scientific accomplishments. Noyek suggests they look for open-minded, flexible, socially concerned individuals who seek to construct a more civil and peaceful society. His partners are 'more than scientists,' who are able to look 'beyond the microscope' to see the social and political context in which they operate.

As the activities of CISEPO operate against the background of long-standing political, social, and religious conflicts, the central coordinating body of the network based in Toronto acts as a facilitator, bringing parties to common ground. If it is to implement its programs, CISEPO must be flexible in the face of difficult, rapidly shifting, negative environments. The first continuing education workshop to be held between Israel and Jordan is a good example of the environment within which CISEPO operates and of the approach that its leadership employs. CISEPO planned the workshop to offer needed resources to both governments – providing knowledge, building bridges across communities, and creating a secure space for scientific interaction that rose above the political tensions in order to improve the management of legitimate medical needs across the region. In a case of unfortunate timing, the workshop opened the morning of a bombing in Tel Aviv. As the workshop was formally hosted by the Jordanian government, and the Israeli academics were to meet with their counterparts at a Jordanian military facility, the Israelis believed they must leave. The Jordanians were unsure how to respond. While the ultimate decision was for the Israeli representatives to make, the Toronto team encouraged them to stay. They did, and, following rapid discussions led by the Toronto team, the conference began with a formal statement by the Jordanian representatives, condemning the attack and sending their condolences to the Israeli people. Noyek, his departmental colleagues, and the Israeli and Jordanian network members had developed strong personal relationships that enabled them to collaborate and continue their professional activities, even under difficult circumstances.

Membership

CISEPO works with leading researchers – physicians, scientists, and other health care professionals – primarily in the fields of otolaryngology, oncology (cancer research), radiology, and molecular biology, but also more recently in epidemiology and cardiology. Noyek and his project directors decide with whom they will form partnerships, but the perception of the interviewer is that membership is flexible and fluid. Noyek estimates that there are approximately 50 core members, 100 peripheral members, and 150 outside contacts, excluding benefactors and patients who support the network. The core members are active participants, in regular contact with other network members. The peripheral members participate to a lesser degree within the framework of their interests and needs. The outside contacts, such as Leo Kramer mentioned earlier, are involved on an ad hoc basis. Membership and participation is a concentric, multi-layered structure.

Of all the networks surveyed in this project, CISEPO's membership is the hardest to confirm with confidence. Unlike GURI and CARNET, network members do not sign a contract outlining their obligations. If individuals or organizations have had sustained contact with members on network projects, they appear to be considered members. Leo Kramer mentioned that Noyek is a powerful, energetic individual who is willing to expand the network 'beyond himself.' Kramer himself is a good example. He became aware that members of the Orthodox Jewish community in New York wanted to contribute to the peace process in the Middle East by supplying medical support to Palestinians. As Kramer investigated the possibilities with Palestinians there, Noyek heard of his activities and contacted him immediately. Core members, however, are frequently those individuals who the Toronto team members know well and in whom they have a high degree of confidence.

Communication

As with one of the other cases in this volume, CARNET, CISEPO's experience indicates the importance of face-to-face interaction to strengthen personal relationships, even within the context of technologically facilitated communication. Though we were unable to measure this systematically, preliminary observations by the network director suggest that in addition to fax and phone contact, and network continuing education meetings, the core members communicate regularly using the relatively new medium of e-mail. Though it is too early to establish the scope and consistency of use with confidence, initial evidence suggests that e-mail is useful for sustaining relationships and transferring timely information during the periods between face-to-face meetings. The director cultivates communication between members but believes that in some regions communication is ongoing and sustainable without intervention from the Toronto office. Information generated in some of our interviews supports this belief. Because this network is dependent upon personal trust, the combination of face-to-face interaction supported by technologically assisted communication is a central element. The Toronto team facilitates communication between network members in the early stages, in order to construct the foundations for long-term collaboration.

Evaluation

As in many of the cases explored, evaluation of the network's activities has not been systematically conducted, posing a significant challenge to our overall assessment of network effectiveness. Clinical interventions, Noyek suggests, are conducted through needs-based assessments and follow-up with patients. Evaluation of the peace-building component occurs informally on an ad hoc basis. Evaluation of continuing education programs is informal, as well; questionnaires may be used, on occasion, to survey the views of participants. On neither the clinical nor the policy activities are comprehensive reports completed.[3]

Products and Activities

CISEPO collaborates with scientists and physicians from a wide range of medical specialties, including oncology, molecular biology, epidemiology, cardiology, radiology, and otolaryngology, to produce and exchange knowledge on scientific research and clinical management. CISEPO offers two scientific exchanges: the Fellowships for Peace Program and the Visiting Professors for Peace Program. The Fellowships program has brought more than twenty physicians and scientists from Australia, Brazil, China, Hungary, Ireland, Israel, the Netherlands, New Zealand, Poland, and Turkey to Mount Sinai Hospital to study, conduct research, and participate in departmental and hospital activities. They have then returned to their countries to implement this knowledge in clinical practice, share it with their colleagues, and initiate cross-disciplinary interactions within their medical communities. Many of these physicians and scientists now occupy senior academic and service positions, several with professorial appointments.

The Visiting Professors for Peace is a new program that brings professionals in health-care education, research, and peace-building to lecture at the University of Toronto. It provides opportunities for open discussion, exchange of ideas, and collaboration between North Americans and leading international colleagues. The inaugural lecture, in May 1997, was presented by Dr Samuel S. Kottek, Harvey Friedenwald Professor of the History of Medicine at the Hebrew University of Jerusalem. His lecture, entitled 'The Hippocratic Oath – the Odyssey of Medical Ethics in Christian, Jewish and Muslim Traditions,' encouraged respectful dialogue between scientists and physicians of different cultural and religious traditions.

The Visiting Scholars Program provides scholarships for stays of from one to three weeks in Toronto. Scholars participate in medical, scientific, and educational activities that include training other Canadian and international professionals. As they share with their colleagues, they develop and strengthen professional relationships while expanding each other's skills, knowledge, and experience. The first program brought together scholars from Brazil, China, and Israel at Mount Sinai.

Following their stay, many participants in CISEPO's exchange programs participate in network-related activities through contributions to CISEPO's research and clinical health service programs. CISEPO members publish collaborative articles in scientific journals and lecture in public forums under the auspices of CISEPO. Joint collaborative research projects that emerge from CISEPO's programs result in a range of publications, some of which feed into curriculum development of university programs. A recent example includes the *Manual for the Investigation of Nasal Physiology*,[4] supported by CISEPO and developed by several Toronto hospitals.

CISEPO runs collaborative educational and clinical programs that include research prizes, continuing education programs, international scientific meetings, and elective programs for undergraduate medical students. The continuing medical education program comprises a series of educational events in Canada and the Middle East that promote basic and applied research, the development of clinical guidelines and protocols, training, disease management, and epidemiological studies. Continuing education workshops held in the Middle East have led to the creation of two initiatives: an otolaryngology project established in March 1996 between CISEPO and the governments of Jordan and Israel, and a children's hearing-loss project established in February 1997 between CISEPO and the governments of Israel and Jordan and the Palestinian Authority.

The children's hearing-loss project developed after discussions between CISEPO, the Israeli and Palestinian Authority Ministers of Health, and the Director of the Royal Jordanian Medical Services. Led by CISEPO, the project's first workshop was held in Gaza in 1997, hosted by the Atfaluna Society for Deaf Children. Canadian, Palestinian, and Israeli medical professionals, together with approximately fifty-five Palestinian health care, education, social services, and government officials, participated in the workshop. While advancing knowledge on the basic science and clinical management of children's hearing loss, the workshop brought together Palestinians, Israelis, Moslems, Jews, and Christians to establish and strengthen their professional and personal relationships.

A second continuing education workshop, held in Toronto on 12 December 1997, developed this collaborative program further. Representatives from Israel, Jordan, and the Palestinian Authority were invited as faculty along with their Canadian colleagues from a number of Toronto hospitals. The workshop, entitled 'Early Detection of Hearing Loss in Infants and Children,' established common frameworks that may be applied in Canada, Israel, Jordan, and the Palestinian Authority. It significantly restructured and expanded the scope of CISEPO's continuing education program. The program is now conducted by a travelling faculty of representatives from each country, who have collaborated on a series of four seminars – three on hearing loss, one on surgical skills – held at a number of locations in the Middle

East in early March 1998. There are plans, in addition, to initiate continuing education programs in a number of other areas of medical specialization.

CISEPO is the Canadian representative to the Middle East Cancer Consortium, which includes Cyprus, Israel, Egypt, Jordan, the Palestinian Authority, and Turkey. As part of this consortium, the network plans to conduct continuing education programs similar to the children's hearing-loss program. CISEPO is also leading a continuing education program on REMSEN (remote sensing for medical services and research). REMSEN establishes direct, multimedia communication links between stations, using personal computers, telephone lines, satellite communication, or the Internet. Medical examinations and instrumentation are electronically linked to the computer, transmitting X-ray images, hearing tests, eye examinations, dental assessments, and endoscope evaluations. Initial projects are being developed on hearing loss and on head and neck cancer.

In an effort to provide a knowledge link between the political science and medical communities, CISEPO has held joint events with McMaster University in Hamilton, Ontario, and the Centre for Refugee Studies at York University in Toronto. Designed to explore the scientific, social, and economic components of peace-building within the context of medical research and treatment, these events have brought together physicians, medical scientists, and political scientists.

In addition to building capacity in health workers, researchers, and scientists, the continuing education programs bring together representatives from each community within each of the member countries. For example, Arabs from Israel as well as representatives from each of the different sectors of the Jewish community in Israel are represented at the conferences. There is preliminary evidence that cross-community and cross-sector research partnerships are products of the research workshops as individuals interact, formally and informally. Because of this inclusive approach, these conferences access the capabilities and draw on the knowledge of a wide array of professionals. They also bring these new communities together to promote civil and constructive interaction on questions of common scientific concern.[5]

Dr Raphael Feinmesser, a partner in the otolaryngology program with CISEPO, has collaborated with the network on various projects since 1990. Feinmesser, an ENT surgeon at Rabin Medical Centre in Tel Aviv, who also specializes in oncology, leads projects that address the behaviour of tumours in the larynx and thyroid. These collaborative projects are funded partially through CISEPO and partially through other grants. CISEPO covered a portion of the cost of establishing a research laboratory adjoining Dr Feinmesser's department and has also paid for the residency programs at Rabin Medical Centre for two young doctors who emigrated from Russia, one of whom is now working on otolaryngology research projects with Feinmesser and his colleagues.

Dr Mohammed Al Masri, Chief of Audiology at King Hussein Medical Centre in Amman, Jordan, has partnered with CISEPO in the children's hearing-loss program. The program provides protocols for screening and identifying hearing loss in its early stages, and explores how best to assist both hearing-impaired children and their families after the diagnosis. In addition to conducting research, the program provides paediatric health services. CISEPO also facilitated and signed an agreement to create a scientific research program between Mount Sinai's Otolaryngology Function Unit, King Hussein Medical Centre's Department of Audiology, and Schneider Children's Hospital in Tel Aviv. The program will provide support service and educational development in audiology, with the tangible benefit of delivering hearing-aid fittings to members of the Jordanian population. Dr Al Masri is a faculty member of the continuing education program in children's hearing-loss detection, as is Dr Anton Shuhaibar of Shiffa General Hospital in the Palestinian Authority. They both participated in the 1997 children's hearing-loss workshop and were also participants in the Visiting Scholars Program while they were in Toronto.

CISEPO also operates the 'Looking East' program, which is designing a screening test for cancer of the nasopharyrnx in China. People of Chinese decent have unusually high rates of this type of cancer. An Israeli scientist conducted some of the ground-breaking research for this test while on a CISEPO fellowship at Mount Sinai. The results are being implemented and further clinical research performed in collaboration with partners in China. CISEPO is also applying the findings to treat members of the Chinese community in Canada.

East Asia has a relatively high prevalence of chronic ear disease. CISEPO has funded two medical residents to deliver medical services at clinics on the borders of Laos and Cambodia. The network also has programs in Brazil, New Zealand, and the Netherlands. CISEPO has not systematically measured the frequency of contact between network members, though Noyek suggests that the Toronto network partners connect research between projects where clinically relevant and feasible.

Building on this foundation, CISEPO established the Middle East Association for Managing Hearing Loss in late 1999. The association institutionalizes the activities of the network around the management of hearing loss by coordinating research, education, training, scholarly exchanges, clinical services, assessment, capacity building, the application of technology, public education, and policy advocacy. The patron of this new initiative is his Royal Highness Prince Firas bin Raad of Jordan, while its day-to-day operations are run by a committee of network members from Israel, Palestine, and Jordan, most of whom have previously participated in network exchanges. To highlight this development, CISEPO is planning a series of continuing education events and lectures around the management of hearing loss, including, 'Early Detection of Hearing Loss and the Role of Neonatal Screening,' 'The Economic Impact of Hearing Loss,' and presentations by three visiting scholars on 'Hearing Loss in Israel, Jordan, and the Palestinian Authority.'

Funding

Since its inception, the network has received funding totalling approximately $2,500,000, while its annual operating budget has slowly risen to $350,000. At the outset, CISEPO's activities were funded primarily through the Saul A. Silverman Family Foundation; over time, however, the Foundation has reduced funding by 40 per cent, as a consequence of internal constraints. While the Silverman Foundation remains the primary funding agency, CISEPO has expanded its donor base to include other private institutions and is increasingly pursuing funds from public sources, including governments and universities. Private sources include foundations such as Temmy Latner/Dynacare, the Shiff Family Fund, other NGOs (such as Canadian Friends of the Hebrew University, the Canadian Chapter of the Israel Medical Association, Bathurst Jewish Centre, and Palestine House, Canada), corporations (such as Bayer, Glaxo Wellcome, T.P. Technology Pharmaceuticals, and Air Canada), and numerous individuals, including patients who believe in the work of CISEPO.

The network 'piggybacks' on various grants. For example, the Temmy Latner/Dynacare funds are given to support the work of Dr Jeremy Freeman, a network member. Dr Freeman directs this money toward training residents in otolaryngology.

Noyek is quick to point out that financial support is not sufficient to sustain a network. Money sustains programs, but programs are not the sum total of a network. People, relationships, and personalities are what give the network life. He suggests it is only when people use resources in a way that strengthens relationships, is sensitive to different perspectives and traditions, and builds individuals up, that a network is sustainable.

CISEPO requires a strong administrative structure to support this incoming capital. The Silverman Foundation has been quite flexible, with few reporting requirements. Though donor requirements differ, financial and research reports are generally submitted at the end of the project, with perhaps occasional current update reports made through the course of the project. As CISEPO establishes a broader donor base, there is a need for more administrative support to manage the inevitable and necessary increase in reporting requirements. The network gives money with few strings attached. While occasionally it uses a 'carrot and stick' approach in order to receive research reports prior to providing more money, this strategy is applied on an ad hoc basis and reporting requirements are not uniform. Further, as the network is rooted in strong personal relationships, the director and his staff must be wary of heavy-handed management strategies and be sensitive to the unique political and personal positions of the colleagues with whom they collaborate. Philip Aber plans to strengthen the policy and planning structure of the network in order to ensure precise and effective management during this period of expansion, while still protecting the flexibility that ensures CISEPO's success in establishing and sustaining relationships and embracing new program opportunities. The network is well aware that success in managing this delicate balancing act will be central to its future effectiveness.

As we notice in all the other networks, the staff's workload appears to be over full capacity. Noyek, for example, states that he works an additional six to eight hours each day on network activities, in addition to his responsibilities as a physician, professor in two specialties, and Chief of Otolaryngology. Some of the activities overlap, so that it is impossible to measure the workload precisely. It is quite clear he works long hours, as e-mails sent at 1:00 a.m. and conversations during his vacation attest. His administrative assistant juggles her network responsibilities with departmental claims on her time, and Noyek's partners operate in the same way. Some activities, such as the creation of the network web page, are completed by volunteers.

Impacts and Benefits

To the question of how the network measures the success of its activities, Aber asked Noyek 'how on earth' he would respond. The network leadership has not systematically assessed the effectiveness of the current structure and management of the network or of its clinical and political activities. Theoretically, success in the scientific sphere is easier to measure, as the network partners have the structure to conduct needs-based assessments and follow-up evaluations embedded in the process of clinical research and medical treatment. Measuring success in peace-building is difficult and contentious. Indeed, the network struggles to integrate political concepts and principles into its operations. Noyek states that an activity has successfully promoted peace-building if the participants are 'still in the game the next day.' A successful peace-building activity has strengthened the professional relationship, producing the prospect of growth and further collaboration in the next encounter. While this answer would not satisfy many scholars of international relations, who often focus on processes at the macro level, it is clear that CISEPO is working with the same concepts at the micro level: on one small piece of a much larger puzzle.[6]

Feinmesser provides positive assessments of his collaboration with CISEPO. The Molecular Biology Laboratory and Cancer Research Program at Tel Aviv University and Rabin Medical Centre is the leading thyroid and larynx cancer centre in the region. Established in 1994, it is a shared vision between Noyek and Feinmesser. Very few clinical departments have research facilities alongside, but Noyek and Feinmesser believe that doctors are more effective when they both understand how biological mechanisms operate and are trained to perform surgery effectively. In this setting, doctors perform both research and clinical duties. They link the conceptual and the operational, the laboratory and the clinic, in order to construct and transmit knowledge to improve the provision of medical services. Feinmesser believes this type of project might have occurred without CISEPO, but he is 'very doubtful' that it would have. Noyek's belief in the idea and his willingness to provide financial support were critical. Feinmesser and his staff won a Government of Israel Award for their research on cancer of the larynx.

The residency positions for the two Russian emigrés may not have occurred without CISEPO's support. The Israeli government is currently unable to absorb the costs of certifying the incoming Russian physicians and surgeons; furthermore, the government cannot force hospital departments to train the physicians. Department chiefs must be willing to accept these professionals into their programs, and the CISEPO program has facilitated the process – at least for two Russian physicians.

An additional benefit of CISEPO, from Feinmesser's perspective, is the availability of clinical consultation. Noyek's department is an invaluable resource for Feinmesser and his colleagues, who on occasion need help from someone who knows more about proper treatment in a particular case. Through the connection with Noyek and his team, Feinmesser has access to opinions and information that enable him to make better clinical decisions.

Feinmesser has also benefited from CISEPO on a professional level. He was at Mount Sinai's ENT department on a fellowship when he received his appointment as Chief of what were essentially three departments: Beilinson Medical Centre and Hasharon Medical Centre (joined as part of Rabin Medical Centre) and Children's Otolaryngology at Schneider Children's Hospital. Feinmesser was very young – 40 years of age – and needed access to expertise. The Toronto colleagues in ENT were invaluable. He states that 'the access to expertise and the opportunity to communicate easily and freely at all times with my colleagues at Mount Sinai has been and is crucial in enabling me to do my job.'

Feinmesser appreciates the opportunity to send his residents for specialized training and practice at Mount Sinai and other Toronto teaching hospitals. Noyek receives them and further prepares them for research and clinical practice. Feinmesser recounts that one physician supported by CISEPO to train at The Toronto Hospital is now practising in Israel. A second focused specifically on paediatric otolaryngology and now is practising at an Israeli children's hospital. Previously, no one in Israel was specifically trained in this area.

The last major advantage of CISEPO from Feinmesser's perspective is the role of the network in peace-building. He believes they are making small but significant advances through collaborative conferences of Jordanians, Israelis, and Egyptians, conferences that cultivate and sustain relationships among physicians in the three countries. Feinmesser has direct and ongoing contact with his counterparts in these countries over shared issues of scientific concern. If CISEPO had not initiated and facilitated these activities, Feinmesser states, there was 'no way this would have happened.' CISEPO made the first step possible. Now

Feinmesser continues to work with his colleagues in Jordan and Egypt on his own, without formal intervention from the Toronto team.

Dr Al Masri is also pleased with the network's performance thus far. It is possible that the hearing-loss project might have been implemented without CISEPO's efforts because it was so desperately needed, though it would not have been in collaboration with the Israeli physicians. He maintains that the peace-building component would not have occurred without CISEPO. Al Masri on his own would not have contacted his colleagues in Israel, but now he is in regular contact with Raphael Feinmesser and his colleagues from Tel Aviv. As a result, he now works with Arab Israelis and communicates with Noyek regularly via e-mail and by phone. The three doctors have established positive working relationships and have developed a mutual respect on professional and personal levels. They now want to take this process one step further. In Al Masri's words, 'peace is difficult for our people to accept but it is best for our country. The normal population on the street must feel the results – not just the professionals.' Al Masri would like to build a clinic or establish a research organization in collaboration with CISEPO as an example of tangible benefits from cooperation between Jordanians and Israelis. Through discernible improvements in health care, he is able to demonstrate some of the benefits of peace to the civilian population. As a previous CISEPO fellow, Dr Ran Goshen, says, 'A peace process only based on moral arguments will not be successful.' He suggests that proponents of peace must create clear compelling evidence that peace is preferable to conflict through practical examples of success in various sectors.

In periods of high tension, CISEPO's activities in the Middle East are put under strain, but the relationships that are being fostered help to cross the political divide. Dr Daniel Fliss, who received a CISEPO fellowship to train in Canada two years ago, returned to Ben Gurion University Hospital in Israel's Negev Desert with expertise in a rarely studied area of skull-based ENT surgery. Also a key participant in the Continuing Education Workshop on Hearing Loss held in Gaza in 1997, Fliss conducts a project that brings together physicians at Ben Gurion and Shiffa General Hospital in the Palestinian Authority. Against the backdrop of the recent resurgence in violence, he has continued to treat Palestinian hearing-loss patients at Ben Gurion Hospital. Often, because of the strong personal relationships of the physicians and surgeons, they are able to work across the green line in times of high tension and violence.

Dr Anton Shuhaibar, Chief of ENT at Shiffa General Hospital, speaks highly of the bridge-building aspect of the network. He was very impressed, for example, when Noyek and Fliss first came to Gaza for a CISEPO-sponsored otolaryngology conference. He believes it was very difficult for Israelis to come to Gaza and is confident in their integrity and commitment to the peace process. Because of their willingness to take the first step forward, he is willing to work for peace.

As Leo Kramer points out, very few people are creating and conducting programs like CISEPO's in the Middle East. A number of groups are talking about peace-building from the ground up, but, in his experience, very few are actually acting on these ideas. Kramer is cautiously optimistic and believes that the network has the potential to contribute in a 'significant' way to Middle East peace-building. Indeed, he is encouraging Noyek to become involved in a possible collaborative venture that would build a regional medical centre involving collaboration between Jordan, the Palestinian Authority, Israel, and Egypt.

Closer to home, CISEPO brings together three of the network's Canadian member organizations – B'nai Brith, the Canadian Jewish Congress, and Palestine House. Representatives of these three organizations have met formally. Finally, an important product of the CISEPO network that should not be overlooked is the sense of community and mutual respect among members which it has managed to foster. This somewhat intangible benefit is, of course, a key to CISEPO's 'ground-up' peace-building contribution.

Conclusion

CISEPO has learned several lessons from its activities. First, Noyek emphasizes that network coordinators and members needed to learn to be aware of and sensitive to the political environment in which they operate. Governments move more slowly in the Middle East than they do here. The network had to learn how to overcome obstacles and persuade governments to support its activities. Once the governments and partners agreed, Middle Eastern partners struggled to adjust to the fact that CISEPO does not bring money so much as knowledge. The role of the network in knowledge transfer was an arrangement different from that which the international partners expected and were accustomed to. Mr Stephen Bennett of the Canadian Embassy in Jordan echoes this refrain. He suggests that the challenges that CISEPO has faced in strengthening relationships and implementing concrete projects has taught it that patience, persistence, and a readiness to keep a lower profile when the political climate is less hospitable eventually pay off.

Second, against this backdrop of political differences, Noyek emphasizes the critical importance of briefing government offices regularly. Keeping them informed of CISEPO's activities and ensuring good name recognition is essential to getting a positive response on potential projects. As scientists and medical practitioners, CISEPO members are learning to be politically and culturally astute. Bennett also points out that CISEPO's choice of partners is fundamental to its likely impact over the long term. While some NGOs might hesitate to endanger their other interests, CISEPO has actively collaborated with governments. For example, in Jordan, Bennett points out, CISEPO has established relationships with the Army's Royal Medical Services and the King Hussein Medical Centre. These organizations look to the Army General Staff and the Palace for direction. In all cases, CISEPO has been formally invited to collaborate with the respective governments in the region. As efforts are made to continue the peace process, CISEPO is well situated to promote, quietly and persistently through the knowledge it generates, improvements in the health of populations as well as in the relationships that it is cultivating and strengthening among Israelis, Palestinians, and Jordanians.

Third, Noyek suggests that it is likely preferable to have a more structured funding strategy from the outset. It is generally difficult, however, to develop wide support until the network starts to deliver concrete outcomes, leaving a space of time during which network members have been required to overextend themselves to ensure the network will grow enough to garner the necessary financial support.

CISEPO's efforts to join apparently unrelated agendas reveals one unique contribution of networks. CISEPO links members from different communities and political jurisdictions to promote a transnational policy agenda in which human needs are respected and given priority, irrespective of political conditions. Because of their scientific expertise and capacity to provide health services, members have the credibility to speak to issues of health research and management. It is, however, their willingness to be advocates on issues of humanitarian concern – to think 'outside the box' as scientists and physicians – that has led to the collaborative transnational partnerships between governments and private citizens. CISEPO works with governments to generate transnational policies around health management while creating the foundations to operate when the political climate may be less hospitable. The non-hierarchical nature of the network structure, rooted in strong interpersonal relationships, facilitates this agility in operating in and adapting to unstable political conditions.

While CISEPO will not on its own solve the problem of peace in countries divided by hostilities, its activities seek to form a small part of the solution. It draws the governments of its respective members into the network and encourages them to overlook sectarian or other political differences and to respond collectively to human needs. The interpersonal relationships themselves create spaces of peace, providing places where citizens of opposing political jurisdictions relate to one another as if peaceful conditions between their countries existed.

CISEPO's success is dependent upon four major factors. First, the medical services that the network provides are desperately needed, and in many cases the services cannot be provided unless members work together. For example, Shiffa General Hospital in the Palestinian Authority is in critical need of medical expertise, while Israel's hospitals are empty. The Israeli medical community seeks the financial gain that peace can bring. In essence, they need each other. Second, the strength of the network lies in its ability to link professional activities and personal relationships. The network views people as a resource, supports them on a professional and personal level, and draws them together. The social relationships that are established and nurtured form the foundation for the medical research and health services that are provided, creating a space through which humanitarian action may take place in the midst of political instability.

Third, the network is rooted in the principle of professional and personal capacity building. In the words of Leo Kramer, Noyek seeks to 'get things done.' Noyek views his role as a facilitator, sending international partners notes and e-mails, and calling them when political and personal circumstances are difficult. He suggests that his greatest challenge as director is keeping the members 'up' when they have every reason to be discouraged. He infuses the network with a momentum which is surprising, given the stressful, politicized environment in which members conduct their activities. It is not clear whether the network would be sustainable in its present form without Noyek. However, it is clear that some of the relationships that this network has cultivated and nurtured would likely continue. Fourth, and finally, sustained, flexible funding has enabled the network to adapt readily in a fluid, shifting environment and to embrace opportunities that this environment provides.

CISEPO is in the process of establishing an administrative structure and related financial controls. Without taking away the flexibility and creativity of the network, CISEPO needs to structure the process so that its benefits can systematically be transferred to the policy level. Further, a concerted and systematic emphasis on evaluation mechanisms is critical. In particular, as CISEPO clearly recognizes, the network would benefit from interaction with researchers on peace-building. Such interaction may assist members of the network to measure, systematically over time, the benefits of their activities at the political level and enable them to develop future strategies.

NOTES

1 Research for this chapter was conducted through the following means: a series of personal and telephone interviews with Dr Arnold Noyek, Mr Philip Aber, Dr Raphael Feinmesser, Dr Mohammad Al Masri, and Dr Anton Shuhaibar; observation of a network event; informal discussion with a member of the Silverman Foundation; informal discussion with Dr Jay Keystone, Director of International Health at the University of Toronto; an e-mail interview with Mr Stephen Bennett of the Canadian Embassy in Jordan; and examination of internal network documents, information summaries provided by the network and the university, annual reports, and the network Internet site. All personal quotations are taken from answers to the questions contained in the interview guide reproduced in Appendix A. Interviews took place between July 1997 and July 1999.

2 Otolaryngology is the study of the ear, nose, and throat (or ENT).

3 Please note: the scope of this project did not allow the researchers to evaluate independently the effectiveness of CISEPO or any of the four other networks. Efforts were made to speak to some individuals outside the networks, but contact was necessarily limited and on-site field evaluations were generally not possible. Nevertheless, we suggest that these cases offer a preliminary foray into the analysis of knowledge networks, illuminating the unique contribution they make to the process of knowledge generation, and signposting issues for further, in-depth research on the implementation of that knowledge in field projects.

4 See Philip Cole, Renato Roithmann, Yehudah Roth, and J.S. Chapnik, 'Measurement of Airway Patency: A Manual for Users of the Toronto

Systems and Others Interested in Nasal Patency Measurement,' *Annals of Otology, Rhinology, and Laryngology* 106, no. 10 (Oct. 1997): 2–5.

5 CISEPO has received considerable attention for its activities in the Middle East. See Karen Richardson, 'Seeking Peace through Scientific Exchange,' *The Medical Post*, 5 August 1997; Ellie Tesher, 'Helping Kids Know No Boundaries,' *The Toronto Star*, 21 April 1997; and Judy Siegel-Itzkovich, 'Canadian MDs Help Heal Middle East Wounds,' *The Jerusalem Post*, 16 March 1997.

6 For a compelling analysis of the impact of the transnational scientific networks in promoting accommodation and peace-building during the cold war, see Matthew Evangelista, *Unarmed Forces: The Transnational Movement to End the Cold War* (Ithaca: Cornell University Press, 1999).

CHAPTER FOUR

The Coastal Resources Research Network

Joy Fitzgibbon and Melissa MacLean

Introduction

The Coastal Resources Research Network (CoRR), coordinated from Dalhousie University on Canada's east coast, reaches out to interact with natural scientists, social scientists, NGO workers, and local communities in island and coastal regions around the world. From its original sharp focus on biotechnical aspects of mollusc culture, CoRR blossomed over time into an interdisciplinary forum merging a range of concerns related to social and economic, as well as technical, aspects of coastal resource management, with a special emphasis on the needs and roles of coastal communities. The experience of CoRR reveals how the network as an organizational form allows, and perhaps even promotes, adaptation and change – in this case, change from a natural science to a social research agenda. In a related way, CoRR illustrates how a network, as a result of its flexibility and openness, can actually transform the knowledge it creates. Within the CoRR network, as we shall see, purely technical knowledge is transformed through the network into a social construct which is shared with, and partially created by, members of the local communities that the CoRR projects are designed to serve.[1]

The contribution of CoRR to the emergence of another initiative, the Island Sustainability, Livelihood, and Equity (ISLE) network, also demonstrates how lessons learned from one network can bear fruit in the growth of another. In addition to outlining the main features of CoRR, this case study includes a section on ISLE: although it is too early to comment on ISLE's outcomes or evaluate its success, its connection with CoRR and the opportunity to compare the structure and function of these two overlapping groups make it worthy of attention here.

Funded by IDRC, CoRR evolved from the Mollusc Culture Network (MCNet) – a collaborative venture that brought together ten IDRC-funded projects on mollusc culture in the developing world. In its current incarnation, CoRR is an interdisciplinary research network concerned with mollusc culture and aquaculture, and the effects of these activities on the coastal communities where they are carried out. Its coordinator, Dalhousie University's Dr Gary Newkirk, is a biologist who, in 1989, was consulting for the IDRC on the ten mollusc culture projects. The idea of forming a network to link the projects, some of which had already been running for as long as nine or ten years, arose within IDRC, and Newkirk was asked to become a general consultant to MCNet, the newly formed organization. The network was given an initial two-year mandate, but, following a meeting in Jamaica attended by all the members of the network, its activities were extended for a second phase.

At the outset, MCNet focused on the technical methodology of mollusc culture. While there was some interest at first in the connections between natural and social science approaches, many of the earliest projects focused on biotechnical research to improve the process of mollusc culture or on designing research to identify and solve technical problems. In 1992, during MCNet's second phase, network members met in the Philippines, where they agreed to broaden the network's scope. As project and NGO representatives discussed mollusc culture and aquaculture, they began to highlight the various implications of this research for coastal communities. This new emphasis shifted the focus from purely biological research to a more interdisciplinary approach. MCNet members emphasized, for example, that each project must fit logically within the wider context of a community development plan. The result was a decision to open up membership in the network to include social as well as natural scientists.

The transition from an exclusive focus on technology and enterprise development to looking at community-based management and a more holistic view of coastal community livelihoods, emerging out of community needs, was facilitated by the network structure. The network brought scientists together with NGOs on the ground, allowing scientists to see that while technical support is important, the major obstacles in many communities are actually social and economic.

Participants in the CoRR network thus began to explore new issues and initiatives relevant to this broader social context: the role of communities in coastal resource management, the policy implications of

resource management activities, and the use, for example, of Participatory Rapid Rural Assessment (a community-based tool for needs-
assessment and data gathering). A new emphasis also emerged on
improving training for project scientists as well as for farmers. When the
second phase of MCNet ended in 1995, the follow-up network took on
the name CoRR to reflect this expanded perspective, and in November
1997 IDRC approved proposals for a three-year Phase II. There are currently three projects under the CoRR umbrella, all directly funded by
IDRC: the Management of Biological Resources in Tam Giang Lagoon,
Vietnam; Community-based Resources Management in the Philippines;
and Community-based Mangrove Management in Cambodia. CoRR
also operates three smaller projects that involve the documentation and
review of marine protected areas in the Philippines; a summer institute
that examines sustainable livelihoods in coastal communities; and a
writing project in Southeast Asia that documents community-based
coastal management case studies on a regional level.

Objectives

Originally designed to coordinate and support IDRC's mollusc culture
projects by promoting interaction and project development, CoRR's
objective is to encourage and facilitate interdisciplinary approaches and
practices related to coastal resource development and management. The
overall goal is to assist researchers who work with coastal communities
on the sustainable management and use of living coastal aquatic
resources, in order to contribute to improving these communities' quality of life. CoRR evaluates new technologies, management methods,
and products for sustainable management and use of resources in the
context of traditional uses and social patterns, as well as with respect to
the constraints, strengths, and economic needs of coastal communities
in the South. CoRR relies on a strategy of community-based coastal
resources management (CBCRM) to empower people to manage, protect, and rehabilitate their coastal resources in order to meet their own
needs on a sustainable basis, while ensuring the well-being of the environment. Specifically, CoRR seeks to facilitate the creation and strengthening of local .organizations to undertake sustainable resource management and livelihood projects, building on local adaptive strategies.
Through its newsletter, CoRR provides methodological advice, access to
information, and encouragement to project members.
    As outlined in its newsletter, CoRR's plans for Phase II (scheduled

to end in 2000) are to continue its previous activities of graduate training, supporting and generating biotechnical research, and examining the socio-economic constraints on small-scale coastal aquaculture development. Throughout Phase II, CoRR plans to improve training for farmers and project scientists; the latter will develop and evaluate aquaculture methods, and CoRR will build capacity among local farmers through training, including courses in Halifax and in partner countries such as the Philippines. CoRR also plans to encourage linkages with other related IDRC projects and other donor agencies.

Governance

Structure of the Network

Primary responsibility for the individual IDRC projects that make up the network lies with the leaders and staff of the projects, located in the national institutions running them, and with the IDRC program officers. The network's central coordination activities are conducted from Dalhousie University. Newkirk's role is one of coordination and facilitation: he visits the projects regularly, follows up on their research, and assists with the preparation of proposals for new research as well as helping to phase out completed projects. He also supervises IDRC trainees at Dalhousie University, distributes a semi-annual newsletter, and arranges visits between scientists in the network. Betty Field, the network administrator, assists Newkirk in these tasks, and a research associate, Veronika Brzeski, was added to the Dalhousie team halfway through CoRR's second phase.

Newkirk visits all the projects at least once a year, at which time he discusses their progress and needs. Following the visits, he prepares reports for the project leader and the IDRC program officer, on the basis of which IDRC reviews progress and gives feedback. Newkirk also provides IDRC with a CoRR annual report, which reviews project activities and summarizes network coordination.

Membership

While an organization or individual need only subscribe to the network newsletter to be considered a member, core researchers from each of the projects form the basis of network membership. Measured in terms of newsletter recipients, CoRR has expanded significantly: in

1989, 150 people subscribed to *Out of the Shell*; by 1998, there were over 700 subscribers. CoRR's members include university researchers, government officials, and resource users at the local level. The network has strong partnerships in Vietnam, Cambodia, and the Philippines, together with continuing connections in Indonesia. Links based on the newsletter and information requests also continue in most of the Southeast Asian countries, as well as in many countries in South America, the Caribbean, and Africa.

Communication

Out of the Shell is the primary continuing mechanism for tying together the various projects that make up the CoRR network. In addition to publishing information on research and resources, the newsletter provides a forum for members' continuing contact.

Network members also share their research and interact with each other at the major working meetings and workshops, as well as at non-network conferences. However, the coordinator is uncertain how frequently members communicate with each other outside of these opportunities, and feels constrained in his capacity to further facilitate contact between members.

Products and Activities

As in the other cases, CoRR's main products and activities are closely linked with the central networking activity of communication. Thus, CoRR's major product, its newsletter, is also its key communications tool. Aside from this function, *Out of the Shell* contains short reports from the coordinator, longer articles – sometimes in the form of research papers – by project scientists, and articles by the coordinator about culture methods, research methods, and other related topics. It also includes bibliographies, including sources of Internet information, and details from conferences.

A major activity of the network is the provision of information by the central coordinating office at Dalhousie. The work conducted during the MCNet phases indicated the kind of information on mollusc-culture technology required by coastal communities, and the coordinating staff are now able to provide literature searches for individuals in developing countries who are working on mollusc culture, whether supported by IDRC or not.

As in the other networks studied, face-to-face interaction is an

important part of the network experience. CoRR holds network meetings about once a year, and regularly holds workshops and working-
group meetings to promote and facilitate direct exchange between
researchers. In June 1997 the network held a summer institute on sustainable livelihoods for coastal regions. This first institute developed
curricula for training programs and encouraged an ongoing focus on
participatory research (PR) as an essential feature of CBCRM projects.
Since MCNet's second phase, CoRR had sought to support this focus.
Discussions with partners in Cambodia, the Philippines, and Vietnam
revealed the need for a critical evaluation of their experiences with PR
to improve the quality of research, refine new methods, and develop
training materials for those working directly with coastal communities. Perhaps most importantly, CoRR members realized the need to
explore the ways in which different social and political contexts shape
the nature of PR.

To provide a venue for exchange on these issues, in August 1999
CoRR held a second summer institute on the theme of PR in CBCRM.
For the first time, discussions included representatives of fishing organizations and community organizations alongside academics, NGO
workers, and representatives of government agencies. Using a story-
telling approach to initiate discussion, participants introduced their
work and projects, raising lessons learned and key questions and
issues, and brainstorming together for possible approaches and solutions to problems. These discussions sparked both observations and
questions on such issues as the following: how to use PR to build
broader social movements; involving local fishers in shaping the PR
agenda; conflict resolution; inclusiveness; and the difficulty of addressing non-cooperative behaviour amongst participants. A smaller group
of representatives from Cambodia, the Philippines, and CoRR then met
and transformed the notes from the discussion into training materials
for CBCRM-oriented PR.

Through the newsletter and meetings, CoRR researchers exchange
reports of technical progress, research problems, and information on
other aspects of mollusc culture. Their central focus remains facilitating the sustainable livelihoods of coastal communities through
community-based coastal resource management, co-management, and
sustainable resource management.

Publications generated by the workshops and meetings are another
product of the network. For instance, CoRR's Festival Workshop on
Community-based Coastal Resources Management resulted in the
publication of a collection of case studies from the Philippines, entitled

Seeds of Hope / Seeds of the Sower. CoRR provided partial financial support to the University of the Philippines for the publication of this collection. Out of this project has grown a larger one – the South East Asia Case Writing Project (SEACWP). SEACWP is a three-year project that documents case studies of community-based coastal resource management from across the region. It is designed to provide field evidence of a variety of community-based coastal resource management applications in different social and political systems. The project began in 1998 and involves a wide array of partners throughout the region, including foundations, universities, a government ministry, an environmental law centre, and research institutes. Network researchers also collaborate on book publications with related institutes (such as the Marine Science Institute of the University of the Philippines). On occasion, these books are distributed to member projects and made available free of charge to interested parties in developing countries. Six books have been published with the support of MCNet or CoRR.

The network provides educational resources for students, and works with students at Dalhousie and other Canadian universities who have scholarships through IDRC-supported projects. The CoRR projects also involve graduate students and recently graduated Ph.D. students in their activities.

In addition, the network trains project scientists, who then, it is hoped, will work with mollusc farmers. In 1988, for instance, MCNet helped conduct the Oyster Culture Technology Transfer in Malaysia. The project brought together biologists to discuss the training and community needs, including marketing needs, of mollusc farmers. The 1999 summer institute was a first step in fostering direct discussions with mollusc farmers. The network also provides occasional member exchanges between projects, when scientists or technical experts visit another project, either to learn its methods or to teach and advise. These exchanges, which Newkirk arranges when he sees a need and opportunity for them, provide important learning for the new researchers, whose training is mainly carried out through these exchanges or through visits to local communities in their own countries. The focus on PR methods means that researchers in fact engage in 'co-learning' about community management strategies together with local people.

Funding

CoRR is funded by IDRC, with contributions from members of $20 per year to cover the cost of subscription to the newsletter. IDRC's original three-year grant was extended to four years; between January 1991 and August 1995, the Centre provided a total of $900,000 to the project. IDRC's funding covers project activities as well as the salaries of the administrative staff. Funds were transferred every six months, subject to the submission of progress reports from the network's coordinator. Since August 1995, IDRC funding has dropped to $115,000 yearly; at the same time, Newkirk and Field began to devote fewer hours to the project, concentrating instead on the ISLE network.

According to Newkirk, IDRC is flexible about reporting require- ments and changes in the projects. IDRC program officers work in col- laboration with Newkirk and the various project leaders to set the research agenda. Budget cuts have led to changes, but Newkirk feels optimistic that the network will continue and that IDRC remains com- mitted to its operation. IDRC's agreement to progress into Phase II of CoRR confirms this commitment.

Despite the diminished funding, Newkirk is not seeking an addi- tional influx of capital. As many members of both the CoRR and ISLE networks are already working to capacity, any additional activities or funding would require a restructuring or expansion of the networks that Newkirk believes may not necessarily improve their effectiveness. It is clear, nevertheless, that sustained funding from IDRC (and, in ISLE's case, from the Canadian International Development Agency [CIDA]) enables the networks to develop incrementally, providing them with security and reliable foundations from which to operate.

Impacts and Benefits

CoRR's Canadian coordination unit supports researchers collaborating with NGOs that directly assist local communities in resolving resource management problems. The research questions pursued by CoRR members are therefore frequently pragmatic, and their findings are related proactively to communities through community-based train- ing. The reverse is also true: CoRR project members benefit from local knowledge and experience, which is then fed back into the network. There is thus a natural flow from the conceptual to the operational and back again. CoRR also links actively with regional organizations to complement their expertise, expand contacts, and advance the net- work's research agenda.

Tim Shaw, one of Newkirk's colleagues at Dalhousie, refers to him as 'a flexible scientist,' who takes a holistic and optimistic approach to knowledge construction in his field. According to Shaw, the coordinator's open-minded attitude to scientific development has shaped the network's agenda and influenced the way it works. CoRR's broadly inclusive research agenda in many ways reflects Newkirk's perspective that scientific development 'cannot be done in isolation from the real world where it is needed.' He believes that 'systems interact, not only biological and physical systems but these and the social and economic systems.' Consequently, Newkirk suggests that 'our precious technology may not be relevant in a complex world unless the users can profit by it and not compromise traditional and essential livelihood sources. The problem of non-utilization of technology is often not the technology but the lack of fit to the user's lifestyle and economic situation.'

Newkirk's intellectual breadth is reflected in his approach to network development. CoRR members include personnel associated with the IDRC projects as well as subscribers to the newsletter. The coordinator consistently publishes information on other projects in the newsletter, allows non-project members to publish their findings in it, and encourages and initiates interaction with other projects, researchers, and donor agencies. In this way, he increases the effectiveness of the network by opening the door to new partners and enhancing the quality of the knowledge constructed.

Recent developments in the second phase of the network illustrate how CoRR uses its relationship with community members to shape research questions and, more profoundly, the lens through which these questions are explored. As Newkirk suggests, 'we are engaged in a global discourse on CBCRM, but the local realities are so different. What may have begun as a paradigm shift towards CBCRM as a means of considering coastal resources management and liberating the oppressed has now evolved into a much more complicated array of options.' Newkirk highlights the need to change the language or terminology used to reflect this complexity, while never losing sight of the main objective of most individuals involved in CBCRM, 'to improve the lives of coastal people.' Improving their lives, he suggests, requires meeting their basic needs, decreasing disparities in wealth, increasing equity, and social, political, and spiritual empowerment.

Newkirk and his colleagues at CoRR are 'thinking outside the box,' allowing community needs and experiences to guide them toward transdisciplinary approaches to coastal resource management. Their methodological approach of sharing stories to bring together similarities and differences in local experiences, and then using this to inform PR strategies, may provide a promising approach to understanding the intersection between global and local knowledge.

The ISLE Network

A major benefit growing out of CoRR's activities has been the development of Island Sustainability, Livelihood, and Equity (ISLE), a new network partly rooted in the experience of CoRR. Based in the Lester Pearson International Institute at Dalhousie, ISLE links four other Canadian universities with universities in the island developing countries of the Caribbean as well as Indonesia and the Philippines. Partner institutions are Dalhousie University, Nova Scotia Agricultural College, the Technical University of Nova Scotia, the Institute for Island Studies at the University of Prince Edward Island, Hasanuddin University in Indonesia, the University of the Philippines in Visayas, and the University of West Indies. Newkirk and Field, the administrator, began working on this $5-million CIDA-sponsored project[2] in 1995, just as Phase II of MCNet (the original Mollusc Culture Network) was ending and CoRR, in its present form, emerged.

Like CoRR, the network's research is interdisciplinary and integrated, with a focus on combining notions of sustainable livelihoods and equity (particularly gender equity). ISLE is designed to work with institutions responsible for human resource development. The idea is to promote knowledge and institutional development and to assist in their effective translation into policies and programs for sustainable island development. The research generated is also intended to feed back into Canadian 'sustainable development' goals, programs, and policies, particularly for Canada's island and coastal regions.

Within this broad framework, ISLE develops the institutional capacity of partner universities through teaching, research, policy analysis, advice, and community service; strengthens the capacity of ISLE partners to conduct research and training in interdisciplinary and participatory approaches; provides a forum for collaboration and information-sharing between small island and archipelagic states; and promotes direct links between government policy-makers, communities, and other stakeholders, enhancing the capacity of governments to make informed decisions. By strengthening professional partnerships between its members, the network creates and strengthens institutional

capacity within Canadian and developing country universities, governments, NGOs, and communities. Improved institutional capacity for
training and research in island sustainable development feeds into the
management of community needs both in Canada and developing
country settings. ISLE uses partner workshops, public forums and
workshops for non-network participants, curriculum development programs, exchanges, training programs, and collaborative research
projects to accomplish this rather ambitious agenda.

ISLE has a program director (Newkirk), a coordinator (Pauline
Peters), and an administrator (Field), all located at Dalhousie's Pearson
Institute, and a core group at the university that is actively involved in
the network's operations. A joint steering committee (JSC) of representatives from the different universities involved makes the key strategic
decisions. The JSC is made up of Newkirk, who acts as Chair, one
representative from each of the seven institutional partner working
committees, a gender and development representative, and a representative of the Lester Pearson International Institute. The JSC's responsibilities include discussing, revising, and approving annual workplans
and budgets, which are prepared by a program management team in
consultation with the partner working committees. The JSC also
reviews and approves ISLE policies and priorities, reporting annually
to the network partners, and holding semi-annual meetings.

Like CoRR, ISLE produces a newsletter (entitled *Archipelago*) to facilitate contact between members. The network also holds an annual all
partner workshop (APW), which brings members together to plan
activities, report on progress, and review and evaluate how the network is faring. After the first APW was held in February 1996, members decided that curriculum development would be the first focus of
the network. The curriculum addresses the physical, human, and economic geography of islands; island communities and maritime cultures; island ecosystems; and governance of small islands (including
emerging patterns of government-directed, community-based resource
management). The network is also working on a curriculum addressing the relationships among gender, health sciences, and island development issues.

ISLE conducts participatory research to develop new models of community-based resource management. A series of synthesis papers
related to this research addresses livelihood, equity, governance, and
sustainability. The paper on governance examines how government,
community, business, and individuals exercise their power, rights, and

responsibilities. It considers the balance and influence of political, economic, technological, and sociocultural factors as well as the role of globalization, economic liberalization, global information systems, and expanded political participation in the context of island policy-making and management. The paper on sustainability evaluates links between biological and social science perspectives on sustainability.

While an analysis of ISLE's activities over the past few years is not possible here, ISLE provides an illustration of the innovative way in which the research agenda on coastal communities and resource management has developed alongside CoRR. ISLE's coordinators have sought to develop a highly structured network with, in comparison to CoRR, an even broader scope, an even more interdisciplinary approach, greater financial support, and stronger coordinating functions that have the potential for closer follow-up and evaluation. CoRR continues to make valuable contributions in its field, but one of its greatest contributions may in fact be to have provided the coordinators with the experience to assist in efforts to create and develop another, more innovative and tightly structured, network.

Conclusion

The CoRR network was fashioned around pre-existing projects to advance the process of networking and to promote interdisciplinary research. It illustrates how knowledge may be transformed through cross-disciplinary and cross-community collaboration. CoRR researchers have explored and responded to the effects of social, political, and economic forces on the implementation of technical knowledge. Through their collaboration with community members, the agenda of the network has been transformed from a traditionally scientific, technical focus to one rooted in community needs. CoRR demonstrates how the naturally porous nature of a network, and the negotiation of the relationships among diverse members, may determine the nature of the knowledge that is produced – and the way such knowledge is transformed.

Its success seems to depend on three major factors. First, sustained funding from IDRC enables relatively effective coordination and administration of the network. Second, the flexibility of IDRC and of the coordinator has enabled the network to evolve and broaden, enriching its research agenda in creative ways and establishing new opportunities for partnership. From the outset, both the funding agency and the coordinator appear to have agreed on a broad horizon that would include social science and natural science concerns. This flexibility allowed the shift in agenda to be steady and harmonious. Creativity and openness are likewise important factors in the development of ISLE, which itself builds on the lessons of CoRR and links up with the original network. Third, the opportunities provided by the newsletter and network meetings for interaction and for commentary on the direction of the research agenda have been critical to sustaining the network.

NOTES

1 Research for this chapter was conducted through a series of telephone and e-mail interviews with Dr Gary Newkirk, Ms Becky Fields, and Mr Tim Shaw; and through examination of the network's web site, and the news-letters *Out of the Shell* and *Archipelago*. Most of the information and personal quotations are taken from answers to the questions contained in the interview guide reproduced in Appendix A. Interviews took place between July 1997 and March 1998.
2 Specifically, CIDA's University Partnerships in Cooperation and Development Program (UCPD), Tier I.

CHAPTER FIVE

The Global Urban Research Initiative

Melissa MacLean

Introduction

During the seven years of its operation, the Global Urban Research Initiative (GURI) was the largest urban research network in the world. Coordinated from the University of Toronto's Centre for Urban and Community Studies, it brought together top urbanists from twelve subregions in Africa, Asia, Latin America, and the Middle East to research policy-relevant urban issues and to discuss and disseminate their findings through meetings, workshops, international conferences, and the publication of research papers and books. The network received substantial, sustained funding from the Ford Foundation, as well as financial support from the World Bank, IDRC, and CIDA. It also received important recognition from academics, donor agencies, and urban policy-makers around the world.[1]

The funding model that supported GURI during its first three active phases of life was perhaps the primary factor in the network's success. As we shall see, generous and sustained funding from one major donor, coupled with the donor's flexible, 'hands-off' approach to the network's operations once it got going, provided a high level of freedom in planning and implementing activities. Other elements were critical, but in many respects these other elements were made possible by GURI's exceptionally comfortable financial situation. The importance of money – lots of money – to GURI's success, underlines the point that the network as an organizational model, while it has much to offer that is innovative and valuable, should not be seen as a 'cheap' alternative to more traditional structures for producing knowledge.

The key role of the funder was evident from GURI's inception in

1990. In contrast to some of the other networks examined in this study, the impetus behind this network came from the funder: it was not a case of a group of people with an idea setting out in search of resources. In 1990, Anne Kubisch, who was then a Ford Foundation Urban Poverty Program officer, was looking for ways to bring urban questions to the attention of the public and donor agencies. In particular, she wanted to encourage the Ford Foundation's regional offices in Africa, Asia, and Latin America to place greater emphasis on urban issues and projects. Her concern was consistent with a growing sense in many donor agencies that the urban sector had been neglected, while high and rising rates of Third World urbanization required a shift in focus toward cities.

Kubisch asked Dr Richard Stren, Director of the Centre for Urban and Community Studies, what kind of project he would suggest to accomplish these goals. She also approached at least two American universities with the same idea. Kubisch knew Stren by reputation, having been put in touch with him by a colleague of Stren's from ARNUM, the African Research Network on Urban Management.

Following discussions and correspondence between Stren and Kubisch, the Ford Foundation provided U.S. $211,000 in 'seed money' for a preliminary meeting in Toronto, in June 1991. The meeting brought together – as one participant described it – 'the potential members of this potential network' to discuss the idea further. In attendance were representatives and scholars from twelve leading urban research institutes in the developing world, along with scholars and development policy specialists from universities and international agencies.

Over the course of several days, the network's structure and goals were worked out; and Ford subsequently funded GURI's first phase. This first phase – at the time envisioned as the only one – was a two-year project, coordinated in Toronto. It relied on a network of researchers in developing countries to carry out a collaborative and comparative review of the preceding three decades of Third World urban research, and to point the direction to a new 'urban agenda.'

Over time, the network grew more dense as more researchers and others were drawn into its activities. In a second phase, its structure was partially decentralized through the creation of regional nodes with their own coordinators. The research itself also evolved: while the first phase was essentially a review of the urban literature, the second phase explored in more depth one key concept that had emerged from the initial review. A third and final phase was devoted to action research aimed at policy reform, involving academics, policy-makers, and community organizations at the local level.

GURI appears to have been a strong and successful network. Its success seems to have stemmed from a fortunate constellation of diverse factors, including the personality and skills of GURI's global coordinator, strong administrative capacity, and a program of high-quality, tightly structured, and product-oriented research projects. As noted above, though, the flow of financial resources from a committed funder was the network's linchpin.

Objectives

The GURI network, as we have seen, was created in response to the need for a better understanding of urban issues in the Third World, in order to inform more and better policies and programs in the urban sector, both within and outside of the Ford Foundation. In addition, as a GURI document explained, a 'major long-term goal of the project' was 'to strengthen the professional skills and institutional position of local researchers.' This capacity-building goal was also crucial.

The involvement of southern researchers working in their own local environments profoundly affected GURI's research product. An underlying premise of the network was that 'developing-country researchers are uniquely qualified to interpret global forces in their own local context and to transmit their understanding of their local environment to the outside world.' GURI's medium – the North-South network – and its message were closely linked.

Governance

Structure of the Network

By the third phase of the project, the GURI network had broadened to encompass four large regions – Africa, the Middle East and North Africa, Asia, and Latin America – each with a regional coordinator based in one of the countries of the region. These large regions were further divided into subregions, each of which also had its own co-ordinator: Eastern Africa; Southern Africa; North Africa; Middle East; Bangladesh and Pakistan; India, Nepal, and Sri Lanka; Southeast Asia; South America; Mexico and Colombia; Brazil; the Caribbean; and Central America.[2] Each regional coordinator also acted as a subregional coordinator, for a total of twelve, plus Stren and his team in Toronto.

The network's primary activities were governed by a set of formal procedures. At the beginning of each phase of research, the regional and subregional coordinators signed contracts with the central unit in Toronto, detailing the work to be carried out: organizing meetings, arranging for research to be done, and preparing papers. Notwithstanding perennial delays and deadline problems, these contracts allowed the Toronto unit to maintain fairly tight administrative control. But once the contracts were signed, the coordinators in the South had a relatively free hand to carry out the research as they and their local colleagues saw fit.

Coordination and Decision-Making

Members of the GURI network unanimously stressed the importance of the Toronto coordinating team, made up of the global coordinator (Stren), an associate coordinator (Dr Patricia McCarney), an executive officer, and, in the later phases, a project planning officer, and a secretary. This team administered funds, prepared reports to donors, managed deadlines, edited and produced publications, monitored the work of the various regions, and organized the global meetings. The imperative of accomplishing tangible objectives, such as completing papers to deadline and attending meetings, was crucial to GURI's vitality, and the Toronto team ensured these things happened. One member of the coordinating unit saw it this way: 'Total horizontality without a global coordination unit would not work; the network members need deadlines, output, meetings ... real activity. They would not communicate the way they do if it was just a matter of information sharing.' Other network members also emphasized the importance of well-coordinated activities and tangible objectives.

As we have seen with the experience of the other networks, the quality of the coordination was achieved at considerable cost. The coordinator, associate coordinator, and executive officer had only limited official time to spend on GURI. Because the 'deliverables' of the network included major regional and international meetings, for which written work had to be completed on time, the two additional staff members were engaged.

The coordinators' interpersonal management function was as important as their logistical function. The global coordinator's performance in this regard was recognized as key to GURI's success and to members' satisfaction with their involvement. Stren's style – and the culture of the network in general – appears to have been marked by flexibility, openness, and respect for regional, cultural, and personality differences.

McCarney, the associate coordinator, was also critical to the successful management of the network. As Stren explained, 'the very size of the network required two people, and two people, in addition, who were not by any means carbon copies of each other.' McCarney, a University of Toronto professor, has extensive working experience with international agencies. Stren found that her experience was 'invaluable' when the network was applying for further funding, and he emphasized her sense of the politics of organization. Stren, himself an 'Africanist,' also noted that McCarney 'played an important role in relating to some of the subregional groups, particularly those in Asia, who felt perhaps more comfortable with her than with me.'

Reflecting on lessons learned with respect to management as a result of his experience in GURI, Stren felt that more flexible membership, perhaps renewing the composition of the network for each phase, might have been better. He noted that because of the way GURI was organized, when members 'weren't pulling their weight,' or were causing difficulties for the network, the coordinators' only recourse was to point to the stipulations in the research contracts. In addition, occasionally members who had joined GURI in one phase of research were 'out of sync' with the new perspectives in the next phase; nevertheless, they would insist on staying in the network – perhaps for financial reasons – and there was nothing that could be done about it. Stren also reflected that responsibilities within the Toronto management team could have been defined more precisely.

The tolerant and flexible culture of the network was evident in GURI's decision-making processes. Although GURI did not have fixed procedures for making decisions, most substantive (as opposed to purely logistical) decisions affecting the network as a whole were achieved through consultation and consensus. The choice of urban governance as the research focus in Phase 2 illustrates the decision-making style.

At the beginning of Phase 2, a meeting of regional and subregional coordinators was convened in Toronto. One member of the Toronto team produced a matrix based on the different research agendas that had been identified by network members during Phase 1, and in this way came up with a set of 'most-mentioned' themes. The subregions had differing interests, due in part to their differing regional environments, and in part to their differing academic disciplines; agreeing to a common focus for the next phase of research therefore posed a real challenge. 'Governance' was not at the top of anyone's priority list; in fact, it was not even *on* everyone's list. However, it appeared in some form in most of the papers that had been prepared for Phase 1. It was also a theme which seemed to provide a strategic and timely angle on a variety of urban issues, and, in addition, the Ford Foundation's Kubisch was keen to highlight governance.

In the end, the Toronto team proposed, and the network agreed to, a Phase 2 research project organized under the theme of governance with variations to satisfy the interests of different researchers. The decision was, clearly, influenced by the major donor, but determined through consensus following discussion and guidance from the Toronto coordinators. The network members appear to have found the decision satisfactory from a procedural perspective, and, ultimately, the choice proved intellectually stimulating and productive.

The process for selecting the Phase 3 research project was similar. The idea to carry out participatory action research originated in Toronto, and while some of the subregional coordinators liked the idea, others did not. A great deal of discussion and negotiation took place before the decision to undertake action research was achieved, but in the end all the coordinators did agree. It seems, though, that not all the Phase 3 projects adhered equally to the 'action research' model, an outcome which perhaps indicates some flaws in the 'consensus' decision in this case.

Nevertheless, network members reported that they appreciated the role of the coordinators and felt satisfied with the decision-making process. One subregional coordinator commented: 'The establishment of priorities and objectives has come mainly from the Toronto coordination unit, but decisions have been taken with flexibility and respect for local problems and differences.' Another commented: 'The principal coordinator ... ensures that no major decision is taken without members' agreement.' Another described decision-making in the network as 'quite decentralized and relatively autonomous.'

Achieving this level of participation was not easy, since consulting with the network between meetings presented challenges. With many other commitments besides GURI, and varying levels of commitment to GURI itself, members were sometimes slow to respond to requests for input. At the same time, many members would have been concerned by any sign that decisions were being made unilaterally in Toronto. GURI's North-South composition made the question of coordinating from Toronto sensitive, and the Toronto team had to maintain a delicate balance between trust and efficiency. Initially, some of the Southern participants felt uncomfortable over Toronto's control of funds and administration, but trust seems to have developed over time. In fact, one of the regional coordinators described the network as 'a rare example of North-South association without any patronage.' Others echoed this sentiment.

Because of their regular travel and contact with network members at the regional level, the Toronto coordinators had a valuable opportunity to develop global thematic and comparative perspectives on the research carried out through GURI. Yet, ironically, much of their time and energy was devoted to dealing with administrative matters – unavoidable if the network was to be sustained operationally, but not really intellectually engaging. Both Stren and McCarney reported that they often found it difficult and frustrating to balance their roles as collegial members of the network and administrative coordinators. Moreover, the time-consuming job of managing a global network took them away from their own academic work. A collaborative initiative like GURI results in exciting research, but the coordinators perceived this work as less valued by the mainstream academic community than individual work. Coordinating a global network also means constant travel, which can take its toll on health, as well as on local personal and professional relationships, and engagement with local community concerns.

Partly in response to these issues, regional nodes were established during Phase 2 to decentralize coordination, stimulate greater activity at the regional level, create a more horizontal network structure, and, over time, to increase GURI's sustainability by dispersing responsibility for its maintenance. This initiative met with some success, but although network members valued the decentralized structure, the regional nodes developed unevenly.

Membership

GURI's geographic scope was wide and its membership diverse. It included men and women, senior scholars and younger researchers, different cultures and nationalities, and a variety of academic disciplines. The diversity and size of the network were its strengths, but at the same time posed significant challenges. One of the regional coordinators noted the 'difference in organizational cultures among the participating regions (including Toronto), with some driven by a sensitivity to deference, others loose collaboration, others structural conformities, and even others detailed contractualism! Probably it is this diversity and the respect accorded to each practice that has enabled the network to succeed.' But the same person concluded that 'the different intellectual and organizational cultures of the major regions have, to some extent, acted as a constraint for the network.' Another commented: 'The greatest problems originate in the enormous geographic coverage of the network, which makes relations among the different regions difficult.' Another found that the 'combination of very senior with comparatively younger researchers was a difficult arrangement, but worthwhile.' Despite the diversity of the membership, the GURI network had a sense of mission, which led to a group solidarity that, over time, mitigated differences. This sense of solidarity was related to the members' shared work in the somewhat marginalized field of urban studies, and their belief that their work in this field is important and deserves to be publicized.

The core members of the GURI network were in most cases selected on the basis of their connection with the Ford Foundation's regional offices, or because they were known personally or by reputation to the Toronto coordinators. The majority were academic researchers connected to universities, but a few were associated with research institutes or NGOs. Dr Om Prakash Mathur, for example, the subregional coordinator for India, Nepal, and Sri Lanka, works with the National Institute of Public Finance and Policy in New Delhi. Alfredo Rodriguez, the Latin American regional coordinator, is the executive director of SUR, a research NGO in Santiago, Chile.

In selecting members to join the network, the central coordinators reported that they tried to include as many women as possible, to look for young researchers, and to choose people with good writing and administrative skills. In India and Africa, they did not find women with the requisite experience, but in the network as a whole one-third of the coordinators were women.

Although membership in the network applied to individual researchers rather than to the institutions in which they worked, institutional affiliations were important in the original selection because it was felt that the researchers would need a strong institutional base to provide them with administrative and other support. The degree to which the home institutions of the researchers were, in fact, actively connected to GURI varied from case to case.

The network had a relatively stable membership base. Seven of the twelve core members remained from the beginning to the end, and two of the five who did not remain represented regions which were dropped from the network.

Communication

GURI members regularly used e-mail, fax, post, and telephone to communicate with each other and with the coordinators in the Toronto office. During Phase 2, time and effort was spent to ensure that all the coordinators had access to e-mail connections; however, even though all twelve coordinators eventually did have e-mail access, they used it in different ways. For some, e-mail correspondence was reviewed by a secretary, who read and printed it for them – in this case, replies were normally made by fax or telephone. Others checked their own e-mail and replied directly. In some cases, e-mail functioned unreliably, so that the researchers tended to use other means of communication. In other cases, researchers simply had not acquired the e-mail 'habit.'

It seems that most of the communication flows within the network occurred within the subregions, or between the regions or subregions and Toronto. Much less communication appears to have taken place at the regional level (for instance, between Eastern Africa and Southern Africa), and still less across the large regions (Africa to Asia, Latin America to Africa, Asia to Latin America), except during the organized meetings. One subregional coordinator reported communicating with subregional partners monthly during the early part of a research phase, then weekly as the subregional workshops were planned and papers began to be produced. The same coordinator reported communicating anywhere from monthly to quarterly with regional and other global partners. Another reported that communication with members of the network in other regions had been limited almost exclusively to the global meetings, while communication within the region had been steadier. The amount of communication between network members also depended on the individuals concerned. One network member noted, 'I am now in regular correspondence with colleagues in Latin America and Asia.'

An attempt was made to use the Internet to facilitate communication. The Toronto project planning officer created a main GURI web site, which was to have been linked to regional sites, which, in turn, could be updated regularly with reports on research, meetings, and local events. But although money was earmarked for this initiative, almost nothing was done aside from the creation of the main site, and there appears to have been little enthusiasm for the idea out-side Toronto.

While e-mail, phone, fax, and post were all important to GURI's net-working, the meetings stand out as the form of communication that did most to bind the network together. One GURI member commented that 'without a doubt, the meetings have been the most important element of the network.' Others pointed out that the global meetings were the primary opportunity for discussing and making decisions on the direction of the network, comparing research, interacting with re-searchers from other regions, and evaluating GURI's progress.

Evaluation

Aside from regular reporting to donors (which, like most such report-ing, tended to be accurate and informative, but not particularly criti-cal), GURI had no formal mechanisms for evaluation. Nor did the Ford Foundation carry out a project evaluation, despite plans to allocate funds to an evaluation during Phase 3.

Nevertheless, there were plenty of opportunities to judge the net-work's progress, and plenty of products and activities to act as indi-cators of success or failure. As one of the regional coordinators suggested, despite the absence of formal evaluation procedures, 'dur-ing the workshops and conferences sentiments about the network have been expressed frequently.' The outcome of meetings and conferences, and attendance at them, the involvement of GURI researchers in local policy development, the reaction of multilateral agencies and donors to GURI's work, the reception of the books GURI produced, and, ulti-mately, the fate of the network once the Ford Foundation grant ran out at the end of 1997, all offered possible evaluation criteria.

Products and Activities

According to one of the subregional coordinators in the GURI network, 'a well thought-out program of activities, sequentially designed, has played a significant role in making the network a success.' In the project's first phase (1991–3), the network examined the 'state of the art' of urban studies in the 1960s, 1970s, and 1980s. Network members carried out surveys of the existing literature in order to identify what had been done already and what needed to be done next. Six key themes emerged from this work and formed the basis of an 'urban research agenda' for the 1990s. This agenda, in turn, formed the basis of Phase 2.

In Phase 2 (1994–5), the network organized its research around the theme of urban governance, with a number of local variations. In Phase 3 (1996–7), network members carried out 'action research' projects on selected aspects of urban governance, involving at the local level community groups, NGOs, and government officials along with researchers. This research was intended to have an impact on policy, and cases were chosen with regard to their potential for tangible policy reform. Thus, through its three phases of operation, GURI moved from a survey of the field, based largely on secondary sources, to the identification of a timely and innovative research subject (urban governance), to the application of research to operational policy aims.

Phase 1 resulted in the publication of four books, edited by Stren: *Urban Research in the Developing World*, Volume 1, *Asia*; Volume 2, *Africa*; Volume 3, *Latin America*; and Volume 4, *Perspectives on the City*. Phase 2 resulted in the publication of *Cities and Governance: New Directions in Latin America, Asia and Africa*, edited by McCarney. Phase 3 will result in a volume based on papers from at least nine of the research teams. Collections of the local research papers that fed into the books were also published in the regions, where publications resulting from GURI continue to appear. For example, in 1999, a volume edited by Martha Schteingart, entitled *Políticas sociales para los pobres en américa latina* was published in Mexico; and in India, a volume edited by Om Prakash Mathur entitled *India: The Challenge of Urban Governance*. A publication resulting from the GURI-related IDRC initiative in Africa also appeared in 1999: *Managing the Monster: Urban Waste and Governance in Africa*, edited by Adepoju G. Onibokun.

On the assumption, as one of those involved put it, that 'because people *should* read them, they *would* read them,' the number of books that would be sold was somewhat overestimated. Nevertheless, in the end, up to 1,000 copies of each volume were sold, and many more distributed free. However, although early reviews of the books were good, reviewers tended to overlook the collaborative nature of the project and to focus on findings for individual regions. According to one member of the Toronto coordinating team, this failure reflects how difficult it is to capture the dynamic network process in a book, with the result that some of the unique character of the venture was lost in publication.

Perhaps because of the limited capacity of the books to reflect the real nature of GURI's work, members of the network seem to have perceived the subregional, regional, and global meetings that took place over the three phases of the network's life as being at least as important a product as the publications. These meetings gathered researchers within and across regions for invaluable academic exchange, as well as bringing in important representatives from other sectors – government officials, NGO and community representatives, and staff of donor agencies. The prominence of the meetings also attracted public attention through media coverage. In this way, the knowledge generated through the network was transmitted well beyond the boundaries of the academic world.

The collaborative, knowledge-generating experience of the network was a particularly important contribution of GURI. It was most obvious in Phase 3, which blended, in the words of a network document, 'an operational with a research perspective on urban problems' and involved the broadest cross-section of people, bringing community leaders, NGO staff, and government officials into the process along with the researchers. This mode of knowledge production is qualitatively different from that which academic researchers have traditionally engaged.

Funding

The Ford Foundation initiated GURI and remained – by a wide margin – the primary funder, disbursing a total of CAD $6,461,696 to the network over its start-up and three subsequent phases. GURI's relationship with the Ford Foundation appears to have been extremely positive, and members attributed much of the network's success to the Foundation's generosity and flexibility. From the perspective of the Toronto coordination unit, the 'hands-off' approach of Ford – who would 'sign the agreement, hand over the cheque, and let us do the rest' – made the Foundation a 'dream donor.' Stren related how, when the original plans for Phase 1 were being developed, the Ford project officer told him to 'imagine that money is not a problem' and to think of everything that would be required to make the network a success: administrative support, travel, additional staff in Toronto, and an advisory committee, for example. Sufficient funds were made available to pay everyone adequately and to cover all travel expenses and related costs.

This financial freedom was essential to building and maintaining the network. One of the most important consequences of the generous funding was that it allowed GURI to bring McCarney onto the Toronto team to share responsibilities with the global coordinator. The generous funding also contributed to the quality of the research. As Stren said, it 'allowed people the time to do good jobs on the papers. The quality of the papers would not have been possible on small stipends.'

The Ford Foundation is a large, private American donor agency which, in 1996, made grants of over U.S. $300 million. Yet even by Foundation standards, the grant to the University of Toronto for GURI was sizeable. Of grants made by the Foundation's Urban Poverty Program for policy research, the U.S. $1.74 million to GURI in 1996 was the largest, twice the value of the next-largest grant (to Harvard University).

In order to engage the Ford Foundation's field offices in the GURI project, as well as to increase the amount of funding available, the Foundation's regional offices were each to contribute approximately U.S. $50,000 during both the second and third phases of the network. However, the regional offices' interest in GURI varied considerably, and relations with the regional offices were not as uniformly supportive as those with the Foundation's headquarters. In Phase 3, particularly, many of the regional offices put up a fight before making their contributions, feeling that the project did not meet their needs, and the offices in Chile, India, China, and West Africa all withdrew their support in Phase 3. (In the latter two cases, the loss of this funding resulted in those subregional networks losing their places in GURI.) On the other hand, the Ford representative in Brazil was one of the network's strongest allies, and the Foundation's regional offices in Mexico, Kenya, and Egypt were also very interested in GURI's work – in fact, the regional office in Egypt more than tripled its contribution in Phase 3, allocating U.S. $170,000 in order to support more activities in the region.

Other funding came from the World Bank, IDRC, and CIDA, the latter granting CAD $60,000 for various purposes, including the development of computer communications. The World Bank contributed U.S. $500,000 for research on urban poverty and social policy in Latin America, and to support the development of regional research and coordination facilities. Although it did represent a huge pat on the back for GURI, since the World Bank normally does not fund outside research, this grant was originally somewhat problematic. Members of the network in Asia and Africa felt that providing new funds only to one region was destructive of the network as a whole, and the Toronto coordinators had to negotiate a compromise in which half the World Bank grant was earmarked for regional decentralization efforts.

IDRC made CAD $100,000 available to each of the three regions in Phase 2 (the Middle East and North Africa region was not created until Phase 3), for research on urban issues and the environment. However, these funds were to go directly to the regions, bypassing the Toronto coordinating structure. The African and Latin American regions produced research proposals which were approved by IDRC, but the Asian proposal was turned down, and the Asian coordinator decided that the level of funding on offer was not equal to the effort required to revise the proposal – a feeling shared to some extent in the other regions. In the end, the IDRC research occurred largely outside the GURI framework.

From the perspective of the coordinators in Toronto, the terms of the World Bank and the IDRC funding did not sufficiently respect the logic of the network and ran the risk of fragmenting the evolving structure.

Impacts and Benefits

GURI provided its members with an unprecedented opportunity for exchange and learning across geographic regions and academic disciplines. It also provided Southern researchers with resources: funding, publishing opportunities, professional contacts, and access to international agencies and local policy-makers.

The theoretical innovation fostered through GURI has also proven to be influential. The concept of 'governance,' as elaborated through the GURI network, represented a distinct shift from the way this term had previously been defined, particularly by the World Bank. Echoes of the GURI approach now appear in many places – perhaps most notably in the promotion by the United Nations Development Program (UNDP) of the concept, as outlined in a 1997 discussion paper entitled 'Reconceptualizing Governance.' This interest in governance issues, and particularly in local governance, feeds into the work of the more than 130 UNDP offices in developing countries. While it is always difficult to trace the precise genealogy of intellectual products, it is fairly evident that professionals within the UNDP were influenced by the work of GURI, since UNDP representatives participated in GURI events and are familiar with publications by GURI members.

The network's importance in the urban field was recognized by its accreditation as a participant in Habitat II (the largest international forum on urban issues since 1976, held in Istanbul in June 1996), which meant participation in the formal preparatory process, as well as in the conference itself. GURI was also approached to cooperate in presentations with other important urban research organizations and networks during Habitat II.

While it is difficult to establish exactly what impacts are directly attributable to GURI – nor is this case study intended as an evaluation of the network – a number of members do appear to have raised their professional profiles as a result of their involvement in the network. In India, for example, the subregional coordinator became active in discussions about the implications of a new constitutional amendment on municipal government. His institution was also chosen as the nodal agency for all policy research on issues relating to municipal-sector reform and state-municipal fiscal relations. The subregional coordinator for Bangladesh directed the National Urban Sector Programme Document, a process supported by the UNDP, involving three cabinet ministers and 140 other participants from government, the private sector, and donor and NGO communities. He has also chaired a Task Force for the Dhaka City Corporation; at the mayor's invitation, he worked on the Bangladesh national report for Habitat II; and he was involved in a prominent 'Save Dhaka' newspaper campaign. In Southeast Asia, the subregional coordinator organized a major conference of Thai NGO and government leaders to discuss the practical and strategic implications of urban governance as defined by the GURI papers prepared in Thailand. She was also asked by the mayor of Cebu City in the Philippines to act as an adviser on urban issues. In Nigeria, the advocacy of GURI and the local coordinator's home institution led the UNDP to include the urban sector in its five-year list of priority sectors for the first time in twenty years.

The importance of the decentralized network structure as a means of using and strengthening the capacities of Southern researchers is acknowledged and supported by the network members, several of whom emphasized GURI's contribution in the context of the adverse conditions for research in their own countries. One member noted, for instance, that the GURI initiative came at a time when local funding for urban research was diminishing, despite the fact that local research capacity in many Third World countries had grown considerably.

With a network like GURI behind them, researchers were able to plan meetings that attracted top specialists, officials, and donor agency representatives to whom they might not otherwise have had access. GURI was also a window on the international research and policy scene. The success of the network in some cases translated into greater visibility and influence for members, facilitating their entry into other networks and academic and policy-making circles, where they will continue to have an impact.

The Canadian academics involved saw the genuinely international nature of the enterprise as a major benefit, providing the opportunity to produce materials with global coverage, to develop broad comparative perspectives, and to work closely with Southern colleagues. Stren reported that he appreciated the chance to work with colleagues from many parts of the developing world and to contribute to strengthening locally based responses to urban problems. 'In the process,' he reflected, 'I learned a lot about regional and subregional differences in urban analysis, and deepened my understanding of the social science enterprise worldwide.'

The network also had an impact in Canada through its efforts to include other universities and Canadian-based networks in its activities. For example, it developed close links with colleagues at INRS-Urbanisation, the urban research institute at the Université de Montréal, as well as with the Centre for Human Settlements at the University of British Columbia. Dr Mario Polèse of INRS-Urbanisation, who heads the Villes et Développement network, cited GURI as an important resource: 'We can rapidly plug in to find a researcher here or there through the network,' and that, he commented, 'is networking in the true sense of the word.' Although Polèse was not formally a member of GURI, he was frequently invited to attend meetings and conferences and to play an active role – for example, as a discussant for papers presented at a global meeting. This kind of interaction is, of course, a two-way street: Polèse, for instance, referred one of the GURI members to the network.

At the University of Toronto itself, the network had a minimal impact. Partly because of its size and financial weight, it was respected by the university administration and others who were aware of it; however, there was little connection between GURI and the university. On the other hand, since the Canadian coordinators teach at the University of Toronto, undoubtedly their experiences with the international network will continue to be passed on in various ways to their students.

Conclusion

GURI appears to have been a strong and successful network that met, and in some cases surpassed, its various objectives. Much of GURI's success may be attributed to a few key variables: generous and flexible funding from its major donor, the Ford Foundation; committed and sensitive management on the part of the Toronto coordination team – in particular, the global coordinator; and tangible, precise objectives tied to real products and activities. And, naturally, the quality of the contributions from GURI's international members formed the indispensable foundation.

Nevertheless, as a formal entity, the network wound down almost completely once the Ford Foundation's third phase of funding, and the leadership of the University of Toronto's Centre for Urban and Community Studies, came to an end in December 1997. This reality serves to highlight the key role of the funder. It appears that GURI was not sustainable globally, in its original form, without the support of another central coordinating agency with further funding from a major donor.

The relatively low level of communication at the regional and global levels throughout the active life of the network was a good indicator that the network would probably not continue to function indefinitely across regions and continents. The regional nodes did not, by and large, succeed in establishing vital links between subregions. As one of the researchers noted toward the end of Phase 3, when most of this study was conducted, 'One of the most problematic elements, in my opinion, has been maintaining a good system of communication between the different groups in the subregions, and above all between the researchers in the different regions, such that when the project and the coordination from Toronto ends, the network could continue in the Third World.' Indeed, communication declined over the final phase. According to one member of the Toronto team, Phase 3 was a 'lame duck' phase. He commented: 'The money is ending; the project is nearly over; and you can see that in the lack of interest in communication.'

The lack of enthusiasm for the GURI web site, which might have offered an inexpensive and relatively easy way for the network members to keep in contact after Phase 3, was another sign that there was little interest in sustaining the network on a global scale. A further problem with sustainability was probably that most of the researchers were already extremely busy: without a well-funded, highly organized, and interesting collaborative project to tempt them, there may have been little motivation to continue the networking process.

It also appears that one person – Dr Richard Stren, the network coordinator – was critically important to the network's operation. The influence of one individual's personality, reputation, and hard work (notwithstanding the obviously vital contributions made by the other members and coordinators, as well as the funders) was clearly a positive factor in the short term, but it may have posed an obstacle to GURI's long-term sustainability.

It is worth keeping in mind that at the outset GURI was conceived as a finite research project; the creation of an indefinitely operating network was not the objective. Yet the theoretically innovative and practically applicable ideas and knowledge resulting from this interdisciplinary and global research model will certainly have a longer life. Whether or not the formal network structure lives on or is reborn, there is no doubt that many of the personal and professional connections formed amongst the researchers will remain active on an informal level. As of May 1998, for example, some members of the network were discussing the possibility of holding another meeting, and several of the subregions maintain the links forged through GURI, in some cases referring to themselves as 'post-GURI' networks.

Such ongoing connections, the movement of GURI researchers – taking with them the lessons learned from the initiative – into professional positions of greater influence, continuing publication related to GURI research, and, less tangible but perhaps most important, the intellectual influence of the project in a variety of settings (such as in the UNDP's approach to governance) are all signs of success. These may also be signs of the particular *kind* of success that a network should be expected to produce. As a project, GURI was well organized, well managed, productive, and limited to a particular period of time. As a network, it was something more: multidimensional, porous, somewhat elusive of definition, but – precisely because of these network qualities – with a powerful, ongoing capacity to permeate many disparate intellectual and institutional spaces.

NOTES

1 Background material for this case study comes from internal network documents, network information sheets, promotional materials, and annual reports, and information gleaned from the Ford Foundation web site. Most of the information and personal quotations are taken from answers to the questions contained in the interview guide reproduced in Appendix A. Replies were received via e-mail and fax (from GURI's regional and sub-

regional coordinators overseas), through telephone conversations, and in personal interviews.
2 China and anglophone and francophone West Africa were involved during the first two phases; the Middle East, the Caribbean, and Central America were all new additions for Phase 3.

CHAPTER SIX

The Learning for Environmental Action Program

Melissa MacLean

Introduction

In 1988 an international group of adult educators met at York University in Toronto to talk about how to integrate adult education and environmental issues. They believed that, although the environment was becoming an increasingly important concern, the adult education movement had not yet begun to grapple with environmental questions. A special effort was needed, they felt, to bring together environmental issues with the techniques and theories of adult education. Out of this discussion, the Learning for Environmental Action Program (LEAP) was born.[1]

All the people who attended the meeting at York were either members of the International Council for Adult Education (ICAE), or adult educators working in universities or other organizations in some way connected with ICAE. Thus LEAP developed as an ongoing program of ICAE, an international NGO headquartered in Toronto. LEAP gained formal status when ICAE's General Assembly, held in Bangkok, ratified the creation of a program on environmental adult education, and allocated funds to the initiative. At the time of the present study, LEAP was coordinated from the Transformative Learning Centre at the University of Toronto's Ontario Institute for Studies in Education (OISE).

As this chapter will illustrate, LEAP's diverse activities and loose ties contrast sharply with the tighter structures and more focused agendas of CARNET or GURI. Observed from the outside, this network's informality may appear to border on the nebulous, raising the question of how loose a network can be while still maintaining a stable character as an organization with substantial goals and products. Is

LEAP simply a virtual construct, floating in cyberspace? Yet LEAP appears so far to have been both useful and resilient. Moreover, it is a project under construction – still in its infancy in some regions, and still evolving. Even though its future seems somewhat uncertain, it appears that there is still a great deal of energy and commitment to carry it forward.[2]

Objectives

LEAP's overall objective is to develop theories and strategies for environmental adult education, with a primary focus on making connections between theory and practice by bringing together 'thinkers' and 'doers.' This objective involves raising awareness of environmental issues within the adult education sector; establishing links with environmental organizations and community groups to help them incorporate an adult education perspective into their work; and strengthening links between knowledge created through practice in the community and knowledge created in universities.

In the 1995–7 period, LEAP's goals included expanding the content and readership of the LEAP newsletter, *Pachamama*; supporting the development of environmental popular education materials in a variety of languages; publishing articles on environmental adult education; supporting community projects; and developing stronger links between LEAP and environmental and adult education institutes and university departments around the world.

Governance

Structure of the Network

The LEAP network is divided into seven major world regions: Asia/ South Pacific, the Caribbean, Latin America, North America, Europe, Africa, and the Middle East. These regions are in turn divided into subregions. Each region's involvement with the international LEAP network is coordinated by a representative of an environmental or adult education organization, institute, or university associated with ICAE. In Asia, the representative is from the Centre for Environmental Concerns, a member of the Asian South Pacific Bureau of Adult Education. In Africa, the LEAP representative is affiliated with the Multi-Purpose Training and Education Organization, a member of the African Association for Literacy and Adult Education. In the Caribbean, the representative is from the Caribbean Regional Council for Adult Education at the University of the West Indies, Jamaica Campus; and in South America, the contact organization is the Latin American Council for Adult Education (though at the time this study was carried out there was no regional representative, the former one having recently stepped down).

The primary role of these regional coordinators is to share with the wider LEAP network the experiences of the organizations they represent. They also come together with other network coordinators to work on major initiatives – organizing meetings, participating in international conferences, and carrying out collaborative projects. In addition, the coordinators participate in setting directions for the network and assisting in the implementation of programs.

A central or 'interregional' coordinator manages LEAP's international activities and networking. The first interregional coordinator, Moema Vizzer of Brazil, played a vital role in the start-up of the network; she stepped down in 1993, and the ICAE secretariat office in Toronto took over until the current coordinator, Darlene Clover, was nominated in 1995. In theory, this position rotates among regions, but Clover has remained coordinator. Her tenure was due to end in April 1998, at which time the other regional organizations and their members were to nominate her successor, but uncertainty about the network's future led to a decision to maintain Clover in her position until the end of 2001. 'Stepping down [in 1998] would have been detrimental to the network,' according to Clover.

LEAP is engaged in, and associated with, research, community projects, and policy initiatives. In many cases, LEAP develops project ideas and works on proposals and fund-raising, but brings in other organizations to implement the projects. Once a project is under way, LEAP monitors its progress and promotes its activities to raise its profile in the broader global environmental community. For example, in Canada, LEAP promoted a 'green jobs' project called 'Growing Jobs for a Living: Building Community Self-Reliance,' near Kingston, Ontario. LEAP initiated the project and found a donor to support it, but the project is actually carried out by groups in the community. LEAP also encouraged OISE to participate: the university monitors and evaluates the project in cooperation with the community. LEAP disseminates project experiences and lessons learned to national and international audiences.

Coordination and Decision-Making

According to the interregional coordinator, her role is 'to keep the thing moving forward and develop new ideas.' Among her specific tasks, Clover takes part in major conferences; facilitates networking within and between the regions; develops research ideas; maintains communications between the regional coordinators; raises funds for the international work of LEAP and for administrative coordination; edits the LEAP newsletter; writes articles for publication about environmental adult education; speaks about LEAP's approach to environmental education to groups around the world; and helps the regions meet their financial needs by assisting with their fund-raising.

Clover believes that having a paid interregional coordinator is critically important: unless someone is actually being paid to put in time on the program, she says, it will not thrive. In particular, it is essential to have someone responsible for regularly providing funders with reports, letters, and calls to keep them constantly apprised of developments in the network. Clover suggests that her own effectiveness is very much associated with her flexibility and personal circumstances. Perhaps most importantly, she is not working at another full-time job aside from LEAP. As she puts it: 'Often ICAE picks people to run these networks who are already overworked. I have set aside a few days a week to devote to it.' Even so, although she is paid for only two days, in practice she works more or less full-time on LEAP, and it seems doubtful that anyone really could build and maintain a complex international network on two days' work a week. The arrangement succeeds mainly because Clover is a doctoral student whose research focuses on environmental adult education, so that her work for LEAP and her own academic work are closely linked.

The regional coordinators are not paid directly by LEAP for time they put into the network. As one of them notes, hours worked for LEAP 'are essentially volunteer hours authorized by the organizations we are employed in.' Another writes that she attempts to combine LEAP work with her paid employment but often puts in extra, unpaid time. For instance, she used vacation time to represent LEAP at a major conference in Germany and to attend the concurrent LEAP network meeting. LEAP does cover travel expenses for the regional coordinators to attend meetings and conferences.

The decision-making culture in LEAP is informal, based on consultation, consensus, and a high degree of trust and horizontality. Day-to-day decisions about how to administer the international network and manage routine activities are left to the interregional coordinator, just as the regional coordinators have a great deal of autonomy in their own work.

Clover says her experience has taught her that it is important to the network's success to embrace creative ideas and 'just go for it.' However, decisions about long-term strategies, international initiatives, and special projects are based on consultation with the regions, although in practice the methodology is informal. For example, at the July 1997 UNESCO Fifth International Conference on Adult Education (CONFINTEA V), held in Hamburg, the interregional coordinator worked with a Denmark-based international NGO, INFORSE (the International Network for Sustainable Energy), on a proposal for a joint project. In working on the proposal, she tried to take into account the priorities and needs of the regions, which had been established at the previoius general LEAP meeting, held in Fiji in September 1996. Once the proposal was drafted, she also sent it to the regional coordinators for feedback.

As the co-lead agency for the environmental adult education thematic group at CONFINTEA V, LEAP was charged with preparing a concept paper. This task, which was the responsibility of the interregional coordinator, provides another example of the consultative style of the network. Clover wrote a draft, sent it to international contacts working in environmental and adult education, and published it in the LEAP newsletter, soliciting comments. Approximately one hundred people responded, and their suggestions were incorporated into the final document.

The two regional coordinators contacted for this study confirmed that consultation and consensus form the basis of decision-making within LEAP, at both the regional and international levels. One wrote that within the Asia/South Pacific region, the Environmental Education Program (EEP) had just established a regional reference group with representatives from the four subregions. The EEP regional coordinating office was to organize it, but decisions were to be made through extensive consultation. 'Internationally,' he noted, 'it is more difficult to be consultative about decisions, but we have attempted to sit down at least once a year to decide on program activities and thrusts.'

Clover feels that the network is more effective when it functions without hierarchy, and she considers it important to view the coordinator as a facilitator, with all members free to call meetings, put forward ideas, attend conferences, and contribute to decisions achieved through consensus. This horizontal governance structure and culture enables the network to draw upon all the members' strengths and allows each member to feel he or she is making a valuable contribution to the network's development.

As in the other networks studied, the success of this style of governance probably depends a great deal on good personal relationships: Clover points out, for example, that although she did not know the regional coordinators personally when she began the job, she feels that they have become friends.

Membership

According to Clover, the approximately 1,500 organizations and individuals that receive the LEAP newsletter, *Pachamama*, are all considered members of the network. Some of them receive the newsletter simply because they are ICAE members, but most have asked to be placed on the mailing list. Many of them send in articles and exchange information, so that their connection with LEAP is more active than their simply being on a mailing list might suggest. However, in manner similar to the CoRR network, which also considers newsletter subscribers as members, LEAP has a network nucleus, in this case made up of the regional and subregional coordinators, who represent the various member organizations involved with LEAP.

There is, it appears, a high degree of commitment to the network. Clover comments: 'We are all committed to developing the theory and practice of environmental adult education. We are marginalized within our own movement and perhaps that has brought us together and made us more feisty.' Another coordinator also emphasized that the network works better than others she has been involved in 'because people see the need for it, and are prepared to put time and energy into making it work.'

Clover believes that LEAP could improve its outreach activities to attract new members and strengthen the network. For instance, she suggests, the interregional coordinator could visit regional organizations that have not appointed members to LEAP, and work to convince them of the value of the network. Nonetheless, there is apparently great interest in LEAP even without this additional outreach. In early 2000, updating the network's situation, Clover noted that the program is much-needed and unique and that membership continues to expand. 'The interest grows,' she says. 'I get more and more e-mails from around the world.'

Communication

The interregional coordinator communicates regularly with all of the regional coordinators, though most frequently with those who have e-mail connections. In Africa and the Caribbean, fax and post are still the most dependable methods of communication. Reliable communication has not yet been established with all the regions, and this poses an obstacle to the smooth functioning of the network.

Communication is most frequent when a particular program or activity is being organized. One of the regional coordinators reports that, prior to CONFINTEA V, he communicated with other members of the network as often as two or three times a day. Another reports that she has regular contact with the interregional coordinator in Toronto, some contact with active LEAP members in her region, but less contact with members in other regions, mainly because they do not have access to e-mail. Communication on LEAP-related business with non-members of the network occurs within particular projects and initiatives.

Pachamama is an important tool in LEAP's networking kit, particularly in light of the difficulty with e-mail access in some regions. The newsletter keeps members in touch with each other's activities, LEAP's activities, and developments related to adult environmental education. As of October 1997, only three editions had been produced since the network's inception, but the publication is sent to approximately 1,500 recipients around the world, in English, French, and Spanish.

Meetings are another important communication tool. Generally, all the regional coordinators try to meet once a year to define the direction of the program and exchange ideas for further work. The regional networks also try to meet once a year. However, mainly as a consequence of communications obstacles, only three large regions were operating fully when this study was initially carried out: Asia/South Pacific, Latin America, and Africa. Building active regional nodes that are well linked to both the coordinator and the global LEAP network has proved to be a major challenge. By January 2000, strengthening the regional networks had been identified as a priority area of work.

The network has three official languages, English, French, and Spanish, of which the interregional coordinator speaks two. She believes that being able to speak at least two of the official languages of the network is crucial, and notes: 'Language is an issue; it cuts people off from each other.'

Evaluation

LEAP does not have a formal evaluation mechanism; however, internal evaluation of the international network occurs informally when regional coordinators communicate, or when they meet face-to-face. Individual projects and initiatives are chosen according to whether they contribute to the overall objectives of the network and are evaluated according to the criteria appropriate to them. Indicators of success include the number of copies of a document requested and disseminated, the number of people attending a series of workshops, the impact of policy work on decision-makers, and the number of people receiving the newsletter. The capacity to receive ongoing funding from a major donor such as Sweden's SIDA, and to access funding from other donors for smaller projects within the framework of LEAP, is another measure of success.

Although LEAP has not yet formalized a process for measuring the progress of network activities, the members are currently working to develop one, particularly because funders want to see concrete measurements of results and improvements. Clover reports that the coordinators are considering a survey in *Pachamama* to determine how many adult educators receive and read the newsletter – but she adds that surveys tend to elicit few responses. LEAP does complete follow-ups on workshops and meetings a few months after the events, and Clover compiles feedback received through correspondence. In addition, at meetings and in one-on-one discussion, the coordinators share the reactions they receive to the network's activities. Clover says:

> We ask ourselves why we are doing this work, what we are getting out of it and what we feel others are getting out of it. We share frustrations ... and we tell each other about moments when we know we have touched someone. For example, following a workshop in Belleville, Ontario, after we had visited Toys-R-Us and talked about consumerism and *seen* it for hours, one man looked at me and said, 'Not only do I have to worry if this stuff is good for my kid, but I have to worry about whether it is good for my community and the world.'

Clover's approach to the development of LEAP is one of ongoing learning. In 2000, outlining LEAP's renewed mandate for the coming period, she noted that perhaps the most important achievement of the network over the past couple of years was 'finally realizing what an international program should do.'

Products and Activities

LEAP is involved in a great variety of activities, from community development and education, to research, 'networking,' and policy activism at both regional and international levels. 'Awakening Sleepy Knowledge,' for instance, was an international research project initiated by LEAP and carried out in conjunction with the Transformative Learning Centre at OISE, York University's Faculty of Environmental Studies in Toronto, and CEMINA, a Brazilian organization that works on issues relating to women, media, and the environment. The project examined educational dimensions of global environmental action campaigns, particularly those related to food and biodiversity, and produced a publication that included comparative regional case studies and conceptual papers. Over five hundred copies were printed and distributed, including copies to all the libraries in the University of Toronto system. Two years later, when no further copies remained and no funding was left to reprint or mail it, requests for the publication were still being made.

LEAP's involvement in CONFINTEA V is a good example of the network's international policy activities. LEAP, along with the Danish-based INFORSE, were lead agencies for the environmental adult education thematic group at the conference. They prepared workshops and papers, organized themes, and held an exhibition. They were also responsible for making key changes to the official document and lobbying the official national delegations to vote for these changes. (The Canadian official delegation was the one that pushed through the changes for which LEAP lobbied.) Together, LEAP and INFORSE were able to effectively lobby many of the national delegations. According to the interregional coordinator, LEAP's activity at the conference was a major success. She comments: 'LEAP was brilliant on getting the documents changed and official recognition for the type of work we do. I was very pleased with what we achieved. It was the first time that environmental issues have been included in these adult education conferences and it was front and centre.'

Another policy initiative at the international level involved influencing the wording of Agenda 21, the document that emerged from the United Nations Conference on Environment and Development in Rio de Janeiro in 1992. Clover recalls: 'We managed to influence the language in Agenda 21 ... we worked hard on that damn thing throughout the Prepcoms, and got about one-third of what we wanted. That took a great deal of lobbying.'

In Canada, in conjunction with community groups, LEAP is involved in the development of a training manual on facilitating environmental adult education and supports the 'Growing Jobs for a Living' project, which brings together the eastern Ontario community of Quinte and the University of Toronto's OISE. In other regions, LEAP is also associated with a wide variety of projects. For instance, the 'Blue-Green Algae Study Circles' project in Australia considers social, political, cultural, and environmental issues in reference to problems of algae overload and dry land salinity. In Fiji, through the 'Saving the Plants That Save Lives' project, LEAP is bringing together women from around the world to discuss traditional medicine and adult education. In Kenya, where women began to burn plastic because they had run out of fuelwood, LEAP provided materials on the hazards of burning plastic and organized a number of workshops for women to discuss the problem and develop solutions. In Uganda, LEAP has provided training to people responsible for training adult environmental educators.

In all these cases, the role of the international LEAP network is to disseminate the lessons and experiences of the local projects to theoreticians and practitioners of adult environmental education around the world – those in universities as well as those in NGOs and community groups. In this way, LEAP contributes to the development of the theory and practice of adult environmental education. Attendance by members at international meetings and academic conferences also helps spread the network's message.

According to Clover, creating and nurturing links between academic and community-based knowledge is a central goal of LEAP. Perhaps as a result of her affiliation with the University of Toronto, the interregional coordinator encourages LEAP to develop connections between the academic and non-academic communities, and, not surprisingly, LEAP's Canadian projects have emphasized this linkage. The same is true in some other parts of the network, notably in Europe and in the Caribbean. The university connection, however, is not a priority everywhere in the network.

Funding

LEAP's yearly budget for international work and interregional coordination is CAD $110,000, approximately twice what was available when the network began. Funding comes from CIDA in Canada and from SIDA in Sweden. CIDA money is a $30,000 allocation from the program funding given to ICAE, while SIDA supports LEAP directly with $80,000 per year. In both cases, the funding has been relatively stable, since it is program- rather than project-based and is renewed every three years. In early 2000, LEAP's parent organization, ICAE, was undergoing a major review, which put funding for LEAP at some risk. However, Clover was optimistic about the outcome and foresaw ongoing funding from SIDA, CIDA, and the Danish International Development Agency (DANIDA).

The international budget pays for the coordinator's two days of work per week, as well as the cost of travel and of producing the newsletter; in the regions, it covers local training, major events, and regional coordinators' travel to conferences and meetings. Additional funding comes from grants to specific projects. IDRC, for instance, provided $110,000 for the 'Awakening Sleepy Knowledge' project. The 'Growing Jobs for a Living' project received a $25,000 grant in its first year from the Trillium Foundation (a public foundation with an arms-length relationship to the Ontario Ministry of Citizenship, Culture and Recreation, which in 1996/97 granted $15.4 million to approximately 400 organizations throughout the province). The project to develop a training manual is funded by a $35,000 grant from the J.W. McConnell Family Foundation, a private foundation in Montreal.

The regional coordinators do their own fund-raising, using the international funds as leverage for further funds, and the interregional coordinator also assists them when possible. The core funds are divided up amongst the regions so that each has between $5,000 and $8,000 yearly to develop the regional networks and increase global participation. The stable funding from Sweden's SIDA, which is ongoing and does not have to be renegotiated each year, is an important factor in the network's success. As Clover puts it: 'SIDA believes in adult education! They are our biggest supporters.' Nevertheless, she estimates that she spends approximately one-third of her time on funding-related activities, writing proposals, communicating with donors and preparing reports to them.

Impacts and Benefits

LEAP's major contribution is its support of the somewhat isolated work of adult educators working on environmental education around the world – a difficult task given that environmental adult education is a low priority within the broader adult education field. In this context, the network provides opportunities to share experiences and develop coordinated strategies that increase the effectiveness and impact of their work. International coordination of funding, activities, and information ensures that resources and information are distributed among regions which might otherwise have less access, particularly regions in the South. According to the interregional coordinator, however, LEAP's impact has been uneven: while some regions have carried out very successful and visible programs, others have no programs at all, so that in some regions the network seems to be almost an imaginary construct.

Clover hopes that eventually LEAP may be able to influence curriculum, and that LEAP materials will get onto university course lists. She also hopes that LEAP's message about the importance of adult education in the community will have an impact. 'Universities,' she says, 'are so "schools" focused when it comes to environmental education, but LEAP shows that learning is everywhere and transformation or change comes from the adult population.'

In addition to building capacity in the South, the network makes an active contribution in Canada. LEAP's Canadian node does not just coordinate; it is part of the network, and engages in the same kind of work as the member organizations in other parts of the world. The Canadian role in the LEAP network is one of partnership, rather than management. The result is that the Canadian universities, NGOs, research organizations, and community groups associated with LEAP benefit, in the same way as organizations in other parts of the world, from the opportunity to compare and share experiences, information, and resources across the globe.

As a Northern researcher, Clover appreciates the opportunities LEAP provides to participate through collective action in solving global problems, helping create common 'spaces' for people to come together and talk about alternatives to shared challenges, and thereby, as she puts it, to 'build on people's passion, power and purpose.' She appreciates the opportunity to use Northern resources to contribute to education and capacity building with partners both here and in the South.

Conclusion

The evidence gathered for this case study is insufficient to constitute a rigorous evaluation of LEAP's achievements or weaknesses. Yet LEAP does appear to be making a unique contribution – within the world of adult education, by working to increase the prominence of environmental issues, and within the environmental movement, by highlighting the importance of adult education. Beyond that, what emerges as a particularly notable achievement of the LEAP network is simply the fact that it continues to sustain itself, despite evident challenges.

LEAP's staying power can be explained by a combination of factors, but a few suggest themselves as particularly salient: a dedicated and capable coordinator, a strong sense of solidarity and ethical commitment on the part of the members, reliable core funding, and a consensus-oriented, horizontally structured organization. Indeed, in contrast to the more formal and centralized networks which, in our small sample, functioned productively during a defined period but then came to an end, the durability of LEAP can perhaps be directly related to its looser structure. The autonomy of the regional nodes, while no doubt adding to the challenge of networking, ensures that responsibility and ownership – a sense of control over and investment in the network – are both shared and dispersed. The decentralized structure also allows space for organizations to become more or less involved at different times, without compromising the overall health of the network.

Dedication to a core mandate with an activist flavour – that is, dedication to a cause more than to a particular project – may also lead those involved to be flexible about *how*, precisely, they achieve their ends. This, in turn, allows the network to learn, change, and adapt, rather than disintegrate, in the face of changing conditions, modifying its priorities and accommodating a disparate collection of goals and methods while still maintaining LEAP as a framework.

Reliable core funding is another major contributor to LEAP's success and sustainability. Initially, this reliability resulted from LEAP being a program of a larger organization (ICAE) committed to allocating part of its own funding to the network, but latterly LEAP has suffered from difficulties arising in the parent organization itself. LEAP did find, in Sweden's SIDA, a supportive donor willing to provide program-, rather than project-based, funds, and this support is an important factor in the network's survival. Still, the network is clearly weaker and less effectively 'tied in' in some regions than others. Much of the difficulty can be traced to problems with communications – the number of coordinators without e-mail access, and the cost of communications and travel given the distances involved. So while the core funding underlies the network's sustainability, it is also evident that more money, especially allocated to communications and administration, would go a long way to strengthening it.

NOTES

1 This case study is based on interviews, e-mail correspondence, and telephone conversations with Darlene Clover, who was LEAP's interregional coordinator at the time of the study, as well as on e-mail replies to the questions in the interview guide (reproduced in Appendix A) from two other regional LEAP coordinators. Background information was taken from LEAP network documents, including the newsletter, *Pachamama*.

2 When the study was originally conducted, between May and September 1997, the network was operating well, and the interregional coordinator, Darlene Clover, expected to step down the following year, to be replaced by another coordinator in another region. In May 1999, Clover reported that as a result of some difficulties in the parent organization, ICAE, LEAP's direction and shape were being reconsidered and she had meanwhile retained the position of network coordinator pending discussions and decisions about LEAP's future. By early 2000, LEAP's mandate had been renewed and strengthened with a commitment to continue until at least December 2001. Clover was to stay on as coordinator until then.

CHAPTER SEVEN

The Canadian Aging Research Network

Joy Fitzgibbon

Introduction

Established in 1990 as the only social science network in the Government of Canada's original Network Centres of Excellence (NCE) Program, the Canadian Aging Research Network (CARNET) conducted research to identify the social implications of an aging population. One of two NCE networks based at the University of Toronto, CARNET completed its mandate in 1996. Network members chose not to apply for a renewal of funding, despite having achieved their contractual goals and objectives. The experience of CARNET demonstrates the need for a less centralized, collaborative network structure with flexible funding arrangements that enable rather than constrain network members. It also reveals the importance of establishing personal networks to underpin the formal professional relationships that structure the network, and, to a lesser extent, reveals the benefit of designing collaborative projects that foster and strengthen this sustained, informal interaction between network members.[1]

Objectives

The $240-million NCE program is designed to enhance Canada's international competitiveness and quality of life. Each NCE network is to generate excellence and collaboration in research, to provide an internationally competitive environment for young Canadian researchers, and to accelerate the transfer of new technology to the private sector. CARNET sought to accomplish these objectives by exploring the needs of citizens in an aging Canadian society. As one-third of the population is middle-aged or older, CARNET researchers acknowledged that aging citizens require new products and services to accommodate their changing needs; as well, they are required to adjust to new skill and educational requirements in the workplace, and to do so while their cognitive capacities change. Workers with family-care responsibilities also confront new challenges as they struggle to manage multiple demands at work and in the home. To address these issues, the network created four research groups to examine products and services, work and eldercare, cognitive function, and the experiences of older workers. Through this research, CARNET provided practical knowledge for Canadian citizens, entrepreneurs, and, where appropriate, policy-makers. In the process, and consistent with the NCE objectives, the network established partnerships between researchers and the business community. The idea was to produce practical knowledge for the country's entrepreneurs, to provide education and training to students, and to create research opportunities for young academics.

Governance

In contrast to LEAP, CISEPO, and even GURI, CARNET was organized according to a tightly coordinated three-tiered governance structure. First, a tri-council directorate composed of representatives from NSERC (National Science and Engineering Research Council), SSHRCC (Social Science and Humanities Research Council of Canada), and ISTC (Industry, Science and Technology Canada) determined the central priorities and direction of the network. Second, a steering committee (similar to a board of directors) advised the network members; it included senior representatives from member universities, partner corporations, research institutes, and the federal and provincial governments. Third, a management committee addressed day-to-day research and administrative issues. Composed of the research directors of the four working groups, the management committee was advised by business representatives from various partner organizations. The network's overall research agenda was established in consultation with the tri-council directorate and the steering committee, following which the management committee established the specific research agendas of the four groups. These groups then refined the nature and direction of their subprojects, producing publications consistent with their established research agendas. The network director, Dr Victor Marshall, was also director of the Institute for Human Development, Life Course, and

Aging at the University of Toronto, which provided administrative and logistical support throughout the life of the network.

The network was composed of twenty-four researchers from ten Canadian universities and one consulting firm. Participating institutions were the Universities of Toronto, Manitoba, Guelph, Alberta, Victoria, and Waterloo, Concordia University, McMaster University, Université de Montréal, Trent University, and Corporate Health Consultants. Over two hundred people were employed to work directly on network activities, including researchers, technical staff, postdoctoral fellows, and doctoral, master's, and undergraduate students. While membership in the network was predominantly Canadian, it had an international component. Researchers from American corporations, institutes, and universities collaborated throughout the process, and the research in some cases included American data. CARNET researchers worked with forty for-profit corporations and forty-five government, hospital, and non-profit organizations.

Members communicated regularly in person, as well as through newsletters, fax, and e-mail. As face-to-face interaction proved to be the most important medium, members met at frequently scheduled colloquia, informal meetings, board meetings, and research sessions. The NCE program established criteria for the evaluation of the network products, processes, and strategic development in advance. CARNET provided detailed annual reports to the tri-council directorate on its research progress and industry contacts in accordance with these requirements.

Dr Anne Martin Matthews, leader of one of the research groups, suggests that, overall, the governance structure was successful. While there were some interpersonal disagreements between a few network members, the Chair of the management committee, Dr Barry MacPherson, played a valuable role. Matthews suggests he was a highly skilled 'arms-length' Chair – not involved in the day-to-day details – so that he was able to rise above conflict to provide neutral advice and mediation when necessary. Further, as the board membership rotated, no one individual or set of interests could dominate the process.

Products and Activities

CARNET's four major research groups produced 177 peer-reviewed articles, 85 chapters in books, 9 complete books, and 483 invited papers and lectures.[2] Overall, the research groups focused on the changing individual, changing work and family contexts, and the identification and provision of products and services to meet the needs of an aging population.

The Products and Services Research Group was based at the Universities of Manitoba and Victoria and led by Dr Neena Chappell, Director of the Centre on Aging at the University of Victoria, and Dr Laurel Strain, Director of the Centre on Aging at the University of Manitoba. Their team identified products and services that would enhance independence later in life. Conducting survey-based research on the needs of elderly Canadians, Chappell and Strain's group produced two studies that measured this population's needs in health, travel, recreation, furniture and appliances, product packaging, and assistive devices. The first study, carried out during 1991–2, examined 1,406 Manitobans and 764 Montrealers aged 65 and over. The second conducted follow-up interviews in 1995 with 962 of the Manitobans who were originally interviewed. This second study expanded the agenda to include medication use and pain management. Researchers then conducted in-depth interviews with respondents from the 1991–2 survey, addressing their needs in the areas of leisure activities, pain management, and bedrail assistive devices. In-depth studies were also carried out with additional samples in Manitoba and Victoria. Manitoba studies identified the ways in which older adults in rehabilitation and assessment groups perceive and adapt to their disabilities; assisted in the development of prototype garments for female consumers; and examined the needs of aging and developmental disability patients. Victoria studies identified the problems faced by arthritic patients, evaluating the effectiveness of assistive devices, home modifications, and a specific treatment called 'Natural Pack.' Finally, the group produced reports for business based on the 1991–2 needs survey that addressed the concerns and needs of elderly consumers with respect to clothing preferences and problems, travel patterns, furniture and appliances, food packaging, assistive devices, and medication packaging.

The Work and Eldercare Research Group, based at the University of Guelph, measured the prevalence and impact of employees' work and family (particularly eldercare) responsibilities. Led by Dr Anne Martin Matthews, then director of the Gerontology Research Centre at the University of Guelph, and Dr Benjamin Gottlieb from the Department of Psychology at the University of Guelph, the group relied on survey techniques to direct one of the largest studies ever conducted on the issue of eldercare. Questioning 5,400 people over three years (1990–3) in five economic sectors, they examined the ways in which people balance work and home responsibilities, the impact and use of daycare for elderly relatives with dementia, and how workers in small businesses handle domestic obligations. Their research included the challenges of the 'sandwich generation' – those caught between raising children and caring for aging parents. The study challenged conventional wisdom, finding that, although the costs and stress can be severe, ranging from lost sleep to lost jobs, these extreme cases are rare, and costs are often less severe. Follow-up, in-depth surveys were conducted in 1994 and 1995. Martin Matthews's group also conducted a survey during 1993–4 of 2,352 employees from four Canadian companies, examining how the employees managed work and home-life responsibilities. A follow-up survey was conducted in 1994 with 231 of the employees from the study. The group also conducted four consecutive intervention studies and one targeted study on flexible work arrangements for those with heavy eldercare/childcare responsibilities. This last set of studies led to a book entitled *Flexible Work Arrangements: A User's Guide*, published in 1995.

The Cognitive Function Research Group was based at the University of Toronto; it was composed of researchers from six universities: Concordia, Trent, Waterloo, Alberta, Victoria, and McMaster. Led by Dr Fergus Craik, of the Department of Psychology at the University of Toronto, the group investigated the extent of changes in cognitive ability, the process by which they occur, and the impact of these changes on the work performance and lifestyles of older adults. They conducted ten major studies on cognition and aging. These included computerized cognitive tests that measured the mental abilities of 230 Canadians of various ages, as well as studies investigating the impact of employment patterns on cognitive function; the relationship between aging and language use; the psychosocial and cognitive function of 71 older people living in institutions or the community; legibility of printing; the retention and acquisition abilities of 116 novice and 81 experienced computer users; the relationship between aging and memory; the relationships between older pharmacists and clients; and the issue of driving and dementia, in which the fitness to drive of 170 older patients was evaluated.

Finally, the Older Workers Research Group, which began part-way through the mandate of CARNET, was based at the University of Toronto and led by Dr Victor Marshall. Exploring the complex demographic dynamics of the Canadian labour force, the group measured the effect of human resource practices and policies on the age structure of the workplace. To do so, the researchers analysed a series of comparative case studies at major corporations or industries in Canada and the United States. In three separate studies at Sun Life Insurance Company in Canada, Prudential Insurance Company in the United States, and Nova Corporation in Canada, the group conducted questionnaire surveys that measured variables related to career mobility, retirement, technology, education and training, and health status, and their impact on the workplace and family. Two other studies examined trends in the Montreal and New York garment industries, with a particular emphasis on displaced workers. An additional study, of 2,147 former employees of Bell Canada, examined the conditions of their work at the time of leaving Bell, and the transitions that followed as they entered retirement or alternative work. Finally, a study of Slater Steels, in collaboration with the United Steelworkers of America, involved four focus groups, six key-informant interviews, and surveys of approximately 250 employees. The Older Workers Research Group produced a series of publications, including literature reviews, secondary data analyses, and case studies.

Funding

CARNET, as an NCE program, received funds from Health and Welfare Canada, Human Resources Development Canada, the Medical Research Council, NSERC, and SSHRCC. CARNET received CAD $5 million from NCE sources and, as with CISEPO, 'piggybacked' on grants from other sources brought in by the individual researchers themselves. The NCE program provided funds in biannual instalments, subject to fulfilment of granting obligations. Contracts established by the NCE required detailed annual reports, which were inevitably large complex documents, while little flexibility was given on major contractual issues.

While the director was unable to calculate how much money a venture like this actually costs, he argued that the $5 million fell far short of the resources required. Infrastructure costs, in his words, 'are real' and, in his experience, significant. As networks require trust, and trust is fostered through face-to-face interaction – not merely e-mails or fax – the network spent a great deal on travel and communications expenses. CARNET spent more money on travel than some might consider necessary, as the research groups were geographically dispersed.

The investment required by the administrator and staff was significantly more than anticipated. The director had difficulty estimating his time commitment, as it was an all-absorbing experience. He was unable to pay for sufficient administrative support and maintains, 'I just about killed myself' in the process. The researchers responsible for the four groups suggest they received sufficient support. Craik, for example, was satisfied with the funds provided for his project. He received a part-time secretary and paid half of her time from other funds. He was provided with what he considered to be a reasonable amount of research money. Chappell, too, was fairly satisfied with the funds her team received, estimating that the $5 million was likely adequate.

Similarly Martin Matthews suggested that while one can always ask for more, she was 'generally satisfied' with the financial support her research team received. She points out researchers also discovered new ways to cover areas of potential shortfall. For example, Marshall found additional support for administrative infrastructure from Employment and Immigration Canada. Martin Matthews indicated that these additional funds were immensely helpful. The money was used to purchase practical materials such as filing cabinets and office supplies, increasing the team members' efficiency. Further, by the end of the grant, the network began to generate its own revenues by producing and selling *Flexible Work Arrangements: A User's Guide.* The revenues from this publication helped support several Ph.D. students while they completed their dissertations.

Impacts and Benefits

CARNET was successful at producing operational knowledge from conceptual research. Craik points out that the network projects 'pushed the lab closer to the real world.' He developed constructive partnerships with hospitals and other organizations that continue, even as the network has not. For example, the researchers collaborated with the Alberta Motor League and a local hospital to examine the impact of aging on driving capacity. The successful project continues to this day.

Strain reports a similar success story. After reading a CARNET study, a Winnipeg nurse, Eileen Ward, opened a travel agency – Vacationcare – that addressed concerns of elderly people who wanted to travel but were afraid to do so because of a lack of medical care. She obtained the CARNET study from the Manitoba government, not directly from CARNET. Surveying over 14,000 Manitobans, the study found that more than one in four seniors had not travelled in the past two years: 31 per cent identified health concerns, and 8 per cent reported the fear of health complications while they were away, as the major reasons for staying home.

Martin Matthews echoes this refrain. At the outset, the researchers' links with industry were extremely weak. Over time, however, the researchers became far more comfortable with their industrial partners and, by the end of the network's first phase, had begun to develop positive relationships. She sees this as an important contribution of the network, and is confident that these relationships would have continued to grow and develop had the network continued.

Chappell is keen on the potential for collaboration between social science and industry, though cautions that this marriage is a difficult one. She suggests that CARNET was ahead of its time in this: social science researchers were relatively unfamiliar with these types of partnerships. The network was challenged to find ways to create mutually beneficial arrangements for business, the academic community, and seniors, in which knowledge generation and transfer enhances the quality of life for seniors, ensures profits for industry, and protects academic integrity – a central concern of the research community. She is quick to point out that her experience in CARNET led her to believe that researchers do not have to 'sell their souls' when collaborating with industry. Despite the challenges and very real concerns voiced near the end of the project, she remains optimistic about the prospects for cross-community partnerships.

Similarly, at the end of the process, Craik did not feel that the agenda was dominated by the business community, and was pleased on a scientific level with the results. He suggests that the link between operational and conceptual knowledge, pushing researchers toward applied research, is unlikely to have happened without the network. The impact of this link, however, is challenging to measure. In the case of Vacationcare, Strain discovered Eileen Ward's initiative through a local newspaper. As she mentioned in the network report published later, 'it was technology transfer without us even knowing it was happening.' Cases like Eileen Ward's signal that CARNET may have had a stronger impact than the researchers and NCE directorate are able to determine. Where it is possible to measure impacts, the researchers suggest that, in some areas, those of CARNET are long-term and cumulative. The notion that it is 'too soon to tell' is reflected in the reluctance of the business community to respond actively to the needs of elderly consumers, preferring short-term profits to long-term payoffs resulting from consumer loyalty. Like Craik, however, Strain and Chappell are optimistic that the network's impact will be seen over time. In some of the other groups, the connection was seen directly. The eldercare group's research, for example, produced a practical guide to flexible work arrangements for the business community as a result of studies carried out in collaboration with organizations such as CIBC, the Mutual Group, and Coopers and Lybrand.

Further, some evidence suggests that this industry-linked research pushed the academic agenda in new directions. Chappell points out, for example, the ground-breaking nature of research from the products and services group, which identified the social context within which assistive devices are used. They considered how these devices entered seniors' lives, finding that users who are well integrated into social networks are more likely to use them. The assistive device study was the first of its kind to be completed in gerontology and, quite to their surprise, has generated debate and is regularly cited in journals and referenced at conferences.

There is little doubt, then, according to the network members, that the collaboration between industry and the academy was valuable. The central issue was one of maintaining integrity in intellectual inquiry. As is highlighted at the outset of this book, it is not that the networks maintain autonomy from market or state forces; rather, they operate in the shadow of them. It is the process by which their relationships are negotiated that may partly determine the nature of the knowledge that is produced. In CARNET, the governance structure provided the academic members a voice in issues of agenda setting and choice of partners, though they were not given as much flexibility on these issues as the researchers in GURI, CISEPO, or LEAP.[3]

The network also helped promote relationships between researchers within their respective fields. Craik points out, for example, that interaction within the Cognitive Function Research Group was very positive and clearly facilitated by the network's capacity to bring together groups within psychology who were conducting similar research but who otherwise may not have collaborated. There was, from his perspective, unquestionably a 'value added' to their interaction. Chappell also reports positive collaboration within the Products and Services Research Group between colleagues in British Columbia and Manitoba.

In addition to strengthening collaboration between researchers within their own fields, there are reports of interdisciplinary collaboration across groups. For example, Martin Matthews reveals that, early in the process, the Products and Services Research Group offered to share additional data with her Work and Eldercare Research Group. Though the latter's project was beyond the scope of the products and services group's research goals, they collaborated. A graduate student worked with the two groups and completed a master's thesis as a result of this collaboration. Further there were visits to Manitoba to speak with the products and services researchers by members of the eldercare group, and, later in the process, they also collaborated with the Older Workers Research Group in Toronto. One postdoctoral student from the eldercare group also came to Toronto to work with the researchers there.

Martin Matthews suggests that one of the greatest strengths of the network was the range of doctoral and postdoctoral students it supported. The financial and interdisciplinary educational benefits were rich. Further, she is enthusiastic about the calibre and intellectual breadth of the students that the network was able to support, train, and encourage.

The research produced was often counter-intuitive. For example, the Cognitive Function Research Group found that older people can learn to use new computer software as accurately as younger adults, and that memory can be enhanced both by specific retrieval techniques and through a process of enriching the information that was learned. The Work and Eldercare Research Group found, quite surprisingly, that it does not necessarily matter whether people are in a flexible work arrangement program when caring for elderly relatives. Rather, the determining factor was whether they were in a situation that suited their individual needs. The Older Workers Research Group originally predicted, based on demographic trends and the prevailing arguments in the literature, that Canada would face a labour shortage within a decade. In contrast, they found that the most important issue was the impact of workforce restructuring on older workers. Further, their studies suggested that early retirement, so prevalent in recent years, is driven by changes in organization and technology, accompanied by global competition and demands for efficiency and productivity, rather than by demographic trends, as originally thought.

Conclusion

Preliminary evidence suggests that CARNET accomplished its objectives, fostered meaningful interaction within and, in some cases, across disciplines, established a foundation for knowledge transfer between the academic and corporate sectors, provided training and financial support for graduate students, and effectively linked operational and conceptual knowledge. Indeed, this network conducted fascinating, rigorous research with counter-intuitive findings. Its progress is well documented in materials completed for the NCE directorate. The research conducted was rooted in community needs. Preliminary evidence of the transfer of this knowledge to industry suggests an effort to structure a practical response to these needs. In addition, the network sought to cultivate positive relationships between industry and the academy. While academic network members were concerned about scientific integrity, they were able to ensure this on the basis of arrangements in the first phase.

The organizational structure of the network appeared to facilitate network development. Accountability was guaranteed through the network's structure, which was much stronger than that of the opposite case in our survey – CISEPO. Again, the importance of strong, visionary, and yet flexible leadership was central. Inevitable challenges in governance were mitigated by the presence of a more neutral third party – the management committee director – while the rotating membership encouraged wide membership participation in governance and representation of a diversity of ideas, perspectives, and interpretation. The interviewer was struck by the candour of those network members interviewed. Indeed, the discussions were not guarded, and all those interviewed expressed, openly and directly, their agreements and disagreements with their colleagues on key issues.

Given its apparent success, why, then, did CARNET not continue? There is a consensus from the network members surveyed that reporting requirements were excessive and not tied to project goals. Reporting requirements constrained rather than enabled team leaders as they sought to accomplish the network's goals. Reporting became unwieldy as the tri-council directorate requested increasingly greater amounts of information. For example, part-way through the process, the directorate requested that the researchers keep a record of every contact they made with a member of the business community – from brief conversations through to collaborative projects. They were required to attach elaborate charts to their reports, mapping out 'progress' on the contacts made. Many times the figures provided were rough estimates at best. While this is an extreme example, the overall process was onerous, sapping the researchers' already stretched time, and quite simply not worth the transaction costs. Network members repeatedly emphasized that there appeared to be dozens of forms. One network member stated, 'I am an administrator; I believe in paper trails, but this was unbelievable!' The excessive amount of reporting created an administratively burdensome process, distracting researchers' attention from the central foci of the project: conducting research, strengthening partnerships, and building capacity.

In phase two of the program, the NCE directorate decided to shift reporting in ways that increased the value of linkages to industry and placed decreased value on scientific merit. Had the researchers decided to apply for the second phase, Martin Matthews believes that the debate over academic integrity could have been resolved, but emphasizes it was a critical concern. She believes that the criteria for evaluation should not have favoured links to industry at the price of scientific merit.

Some members suggested the level of funding constrained the network. As Marshall proposes, 'to build a strong network you need strong nodes, and to build strong nodes, you need an infrastructure to support those nodes.' Given the nature of the reporting requirements, significant resources were required from the NCE program to build and sustain the necessary administrative infrastructure. Funding was to be kept at the same level for the second round, while reporting requirements would be greater. The increasing premium placed on industry contacts to the detriment of scientific merit was central to this change in reporting requirements.

Compared to our other networks, however, CARNET was very well funded, and Martin Matthews suggests that the issue of funding could have been overcome. CARNET seemed, instead, to lack the loyalty of some network members when they had difficulties with the funding and reporting arrangements. Why this lack of loyalty? Craik suggests that networks tend to be more effective when all parties must work together in order to solve an overarching, shared problem. Cross-disciplinary work between interested communities is challenging at best. You need to need each other. This was not always the case in CARNET. Craik pointed out that the selling point for him to join the network was the opportunity to integrate sociologists and psychologists. Overall, although CARNET conducted practical, interesting, and valuable research, it did not function as a totally coherent network. It was not fully integrated, perhaps in part because of insufficient infra-structure and the corresponding need for more resources, but in part also because members did not need each other to address a common research project. CARNET was a network of experts engaged in re-search on aging, but there was no common research problem that demanded collaborative efforts.

However, Martin Matthews suggests another possible explanation. She agrees CARNET did not function as a fully integrated network, but proposes that the groups were, indeed, starting to coalesce. She indicates CARNET was far more integrated than other networks within which she has worked. She points out that networks, particu-larly large ones like CARNET, with broad complementary but not fully collaborative research agendas, require long time horizons to 'gel.' In other words, consistent with the experience of CISEPO, the network structure needs either to start out with, or to develop, strong personal relationships that sustain collaboration when operational difficulties arise. She was convinced that, had the decision to reapply for funding been made a year later, it would have been a different one. At the time the decision was made, the network members were at the lowest point of the three years. She saw, however, enormous potential for inter-disciplinary research and cross-community interaction. There was, even at that point, far more cross-fertilization than she normally sees in other research projects. She believes that the problems and differences could have been resolved and reconciled. In many ways, Martin Matthews sees CARNET as a lost opportunity. Some members would have left the network, but others suggested that, had the decision by the director been to continue, they would have applied for the next round.[4]

Indeed, Martin Matthews was 'thunderstruck' by the decision to discontinue the network. The other team members made the decision while she was attending a conference in the United Kingdom. She carefully, but emphatically, states that she was 'not supportive of the decision they made.' According to network members, the feedback CARNET received from SSHRC and the tri-council directorate was very positive. The choice of this network not to continue appears to result from an unfortunate combination of conditions. Onerous and worrisome reporting requirements that frustrated rather than facili-tated, coupled with too short a timeline to determine reapplication, led to, perhaps, a premature decision.

The lessons here are critical ones for those conducting network-based research, and for the agencies that fund them. It leads to the question of when is a network too centralized? The researchers did not need the network structure academically in order to pursue their preferred areas of interests. The structure was nevertheless helpful, and provided them with much-desired added value. Despite some of the comments to the contrary, CARNET researchers may also, quite surprisingly, have not needed it financially either. Overall, as in all our cases, CARNET researchers are strong, well-respected academics who are capable of generating funds for their preferred areas of research, *independently of the network*. Presumably, these are the types of researchers that funding agencies prefer to support because of the quality and reliability of their research. CARNET reveals, however, that funding agencies need to find a delicate balance between providing researchers with sufficient flexibility in direction and reporting requirements, and establishing those reporting requirements necessary to monitor network effectiveness. Optimally, and in contrast to hierarchical forms of organization, networks are nimble – allowing for innovative shifts in relationships and agendas. In contrast to CARNET's centralized, tightly administered structure, GURI's flexible funding arrangements demonstrate the way in which a more collaborative relationship with the funder may enable rather than constrain these shifts. Researchers will choose carefully the funding and administrative arrangements that maximize their professional effectiveness and productivity. Many of these researchers are apparently willing to sacrifice some of their research projects, if necessary, to avoid sacrificing the scientific integrity of these projects, and to avoid dealing with funding arrangements that strain one of the resources they lack – time.

In addition, CARNET demonstrates that, in cases where large networks are created around disparate projects, it is essential that funders and members alike be realistic about the amount of time required for the network relationships to take root. This requires the influx of capital over a longer period of time before evaluating the network's future, and it demands of the network members a long-term commitment. The alternative is to design programs that require researchers from a variety disciplines to work on the same projects, rather than structuring and coordinating projects around disciplinary divisions. Though CARNET produced highly valuable research, and promoted industry initiatives rooted in community needs, this appears not to be a sufficient condition for network success. CARNET's experience suggests that a collaborative relationship with the funder that includes sustained, generous, and flexible funding as well as long-term commitments to ensure that network relationships take root, may be necessary conditions for a network's continuation and success.

NOTES

1 Research for this chapter was based on personal interviews with Dr Victor Marshall and Dr Fergus Craik, telephone interviews with Dr Anne Martin Matthews, Dr Laurel Strain, and Dr Neena Chappell, and on a network document *Into the Age of Aging: Selected Findings* (Toronto, 1996). Interviews were conducted between August 1997 and May 1999. All quotations are taken from answers to the questions contained in the interview guide reproduced in Appendix A.
2 CARNET research refers to that produced by the four main research groups comprising the network. These were collaborative initiatives with CARNET members over the life of the network. These figures do not include network-related research, although it was sometimes a challenge to classify the differences. Generally speaking, CARNET research and activities were those conducted by CARNET members on projects sponsored and determined by the steering committee and tri-council directorate.
3 I am indebted to Dr Ronald Manzer for his comments early in my research that encouraged me to look at the relationship between networks, markets, and hierarchies (correspondence, Dr Ronald Manzer, University of Toronto, December 1997 and April 1998).
4 Network respondents suggested that because of funding uncertainties and the short timeline prior to reapplication, it was difficult to gain support for projects and to evaluate them.

CHAPTER EIGHT

Knowledge Networks and New Approaches to 'Development'

Richard Stren

The Blurring of 'North' and 'South'

It is more than a coincidence that, as networks are becoming 'the predominant organizational form' for North-South collaboration in research and development, the larger relationship between the North and the South is also changing. On the one hand, factors connected with globalization seem to diminish the degree to which nation-states – in both the North and the South – are able to control economic and social activity within their own borders. Manuel Castells attributes much of the weakening of the power of the national state to global processes beyond the control of the state: 'The nation-state is increasingly powerless in controlling monetary policy, deciding its budget, organizing production and trade, collecting its corporate taxes, and fulfilling its commitments to provide social benefits. In sum, it has lost most of its economic power, albeit it still has some regulatory capacity and relative control over its subjects.'[1]

Associated with these institutional trends are attitudinal changes among the public in most Western countries – lower levels of respect and deference for national political leaders and institutions, and a declining willingness in many countries to pay taxes and to support a broad range of national functions and policies.[2] Based on a systematic overview of public opinion surveys from the 1960s through the 1990s, a definitive study of the trilateral countries (Japan and the major countries of Western Europe and North America) demonstrates that 'most citizens ... have become more distrustful of politicians, more skeptical about political parties, and significantly less confident in their parliament and other political institutions.'[3] While support for national institutions has declined, local institutions show increasing resilience. In the United States, for example, polls routinely show that people have more trust in their local institutions than in those of their federal government.[4] At the same time, surveys show a new interest in civil society and non-traditional political activities and a new relationship between civil society and government.[5] This new relationship is both more interactive and more open-ended. Horizontal, rather than traditional, hierarchical values increasingly influence political activity, and what is local is becoming more important in many areas of politics and culture.

While the nation-state shares power with civil society and an emergent localism, there is a dispersion of sources of power internationally. The end of the Cold War and the emergence of new regions of economic initiative have deconcentrated power globally so that many more state and non-state actors play an active role in international decision-making. Earlier, we discussed the emergence of a global civil society, and of powerful formal and informal networks that deal with important issues of global public policy.

Traditional boundaries between 'North' and 'South' are eroding and losing much of their meaning. Concepts of development, for example, are being challenged from both the right and the left. From the left comes the critique that development and the 'development industry' reflect a model of economic activity that permits control by international agencies and transnational capital over both the discourse and content of major dimensions of political and economic structures in the South. One important answer to this problematic is the 'unmaking' of the dominant development discourse on the part of intellectuals in the North and local communities in the South, to be replaced by particular cultural and conjunctural understandings which give real voice to local experience.[6] Another critique, from a more sociological perspective, criticizes the power and privileges which the 'lords of poverty' or 'aristocracy of mercy' (bureaucrats from United Nations agencies, the World Bank, and bilateral agencies) enjoy in relation to their more bereft colleagues working in NGOs.[7] The contrast is even more extreme if one compares Northern 'experts' to the poor peasants and urban dwellers whom development aid is intended to benefit. Robert Chambers – a rural development expert – has brilliantly demonstrated how failures in development relate to the sharp disconnection between professionals (usually male, highly educated, and Northern) and local people (more often poor women, with little formal education, living in Southern locations). While the professionals (or 'uppers' as he calls them) live in a world of hierarchy and simplistic standardization, often severely bounded by the discourse of their academic disciplines, the people whom their plans are intended to help live in an intensely local, complex, diverse, dynamic, and unpredictable world.[8] From the right comes the notion that all states must organize themselves according to a generalized neo-liberal model of economic development (reduced government, lower taxes, fewer constraints on private economic activity), whether they are located in the relatively affluent North or the relatively impoverished South. Perhaps common to both is the emerging idea that 'development' no longer represents a model whose preconditions or historical precursors have an invariant quality, such that they can be prescribed in all, or even most, cases. Not only is the definition of 'development' contested among international agencies – for example, the World Bank concentrates on 'economic' development, the United Nations Development Program (UNDP) has proposed the more inclusive notion of 'human' development, the United Nations Environment Program (UNEP) and a number of other bilateral agencies speak of 'sustainable' development, and the United Nations Research Institute for Social Development (UNRISD) promotes 'social' development – but it is increasingly recognized that progress in one sector or local jurisdiction may not mean progress in others.

The application of concepts is also less tied to their geographical origin than it was in the past and increasingly crosses the North-South divide. Concepts of development, or of social movements, decentralization, and democratization are much less dependent than in the past on whether they are being applied in 'developing countries' or in more affluent countries, and much more dependent on the particular context. For example, in proposing solutions to the failures in development which he has identified, Chambers suggests a much more equal interaction, with markedly less hierarchy, between Northern professionals and Southern practitioners. In his schema, Northerners learn more from their poor clients in the South than their clients can learn from the outdated and inappropriate knowledge purveyed by Northern assistance agencies.[9] In contemporary social science, comparisons more and more include examples from both the North and the South, and allow – even anticipate – the possibility that concepts developed and applied in the South will have significant relevance to the North. One of the central premises of the 'decentralized cooperation' approach to development – in which cities or local governments in the North network directly with their counterparts in the South without directly involving national governments – is that municipal officials in Northern cities can enrich their technical and professional competence and learn from the experience of their Southern partners. The new constitutions of Brazil and South Africa, for example, offer useful ideas to Northern states about possible reforms relevant to their problems. In his best-selling book, *Megatrends Asia* (written before the recent economic downturn in that region), John Naisbitt illustrates eight new directions in social and economic organization: from nation-states to networks; from traditions to options; from export-led to consumer-driven economies; from government-controlled to market-driven economies; from farms to supercities; from labour-intensive industry to high technology; from male dominance to the emergence of women; and from Western to Eastern cultural dominance. These generalized changes may or may not be valid across individual countries and regions, but the North ought to be 'willing to join in a new world where collaboration replaces domination, and where diversity and convergence are far more attractive alternatives to homogeneity.'[10]

The current convergence of development ideas between the North and South, in contrast to the sharp separation of the consideration of Northern and Southern development in the 1960s and 1970s, both contributes to and is a consequence of the spread of knowledge-based networks. As networks horizontalize and democratize the processes of concept construction, operationalization, and research, they erode traditional hierarchies of knowledge and expertise, much of which was formerly 'headquartered' in the North, and make it easier to encourage a freer flow of new and innovative ideas across national boundaries, across disciplines, and between researchers and practitioners. The freer and more ample flows of information reinforce these trends, as Southern researchers and activists become more aware of trends in the North and as, at the same time, Northern institutions become more involved with Southern partners in both trade and the promotion of development. Worldwide movements such as the environmental and human rights movements bring activists in the North and the South closer together to develop and apply concepts and ideas. At the same time, the network model of organization stresses the importance of local context and the necessity of keeping a respectful distance between what is global and international, and what is local and culturally specific.

Surprisingly, the more open-ended approach to development that is the hallmark of the network model is increasingly shared by international donor organizations. For many years, for example, the World

Bank was considered a hierarchical, relatively centralized organization. As recently as 1997, an experienced observer could write:

> [In terms of] the Bank's internal *modus operandi*, the most significant characteristic that strikes one is its highly centralized structure. Only in a very few borrower countries does the Bank have full-fledged resident missions, and, even in such cases, the substantive decision-making locus for new commitments and policy advice is located principally in Washington. The Volcker Commission found that the typical World Bank staff member spends only 7 per cent of her time on recipient country contacts ... While the Bank preaches decentralization in the context of 'governance,' it clearly does not practice it.[11]

Other observers, some of whom had worked within the Bank, have commented on 'bureaucratic gridlock,' 'generally poor management ... compounded by the excessively legalistic manner in which much of the work is done,'[12] and on a lack of transparency and accountability.[13] Since the appointment of James Wolfensohn as president in 1995, however, the Bank has committed itself to make more of its reports available to the public through an expanded publications program and the Internet, to work in partnership with civil society groups, and to decentralize its operations in order to give more power to the resident missions. 'For us in the development business,' Wolfensohn has said,

> it is crucial to be able to listen to civil society, to learn from it, and to work with it in order to make our efforts effective. There are literally hundreds of thousands, if not millions, of people in the world engaged in development on a voluntary and civic basis. This is not just a group of people who criticize the Bank or the bilaterals; these are committed individuals who are part of the community. And while they may be part of international NGOs, the great majority of them are local. So there is a whole new dimension to the Bank; no longer alone on Mount Olympus – as it was fifty years ago after World War II – but part of an expanding universe of bilateral, regional, and multilateral institutions. Multilateral lending is now dwarfed in terms of available funds by the private sector and literally hundreds of thousands of individuals contributing from civil society.[14]

In a well-publicized evaluation of the perception of the Bank's success in working with the development community in donor countries, it was reported in 1998 that 'there is a clear acknowledgment among

NGO respondents of a more open dialogue with the Bank and a concerted effort by the Bank to improve its outreach among the NGO community.'[15]

As the World Bank changes its approach to civil society, it also appears to be changing its approach to research and knowledge production. Its president says the Bank is to be 'a knowledge institution,' which will both produce knowledge and help its partners to link with other institutions that can disseminate knowledge.[16] In a recent issue of its *World Development Report* (for 1998/99), the Bank focuses on the theme of 'Knowledge for Development.' In arguing that research and project evaluation are important constituents of economic success, the report suggests that 'local knowledge creation – and its transfer from one country to another – ... has the potential to unleash powerful development forces.'[17] While it admits that the impact of this knowledge creation and dissemination is difficult to measure, the Bank has found that what it calls 'analytical work' on projects – writing economic memoranda, carrying out poverty assessments, and writing reports – improves project performance:

> Indeed, one additional week of analytical work by World Bank staff increases the benefits of an average-size Bank-financed project by four to eight times the cost of that week of staff time. And because analytical work typically relates to more than one project, the overall benefit is even larger: up to twelve to fifteen times the cost. Moreover, these are just the benefits to projects financed by the Bank. If the changes inspired by the Bank's analysis affect other donor-financed projects, or even perhaps all government projects as well as policies, the returns to analytical work could be truly astronomical.[18]

That there is an emerging conceptual convergence between North and South is clearly evident in the cases considered in this study. In the Visiting Professors for Peace Program of the CISEPO network, physicians and scientists from ten countries have visited Canada to participate in scientific activities; and a group of physicians from Jordan, Israel, and Palestine were brought to Toronto to design a program on child hearing-loss detection for application in the Palestinian Authority, Canada, and the other two countries. By translating professional activities into personal relationships, the CISEPO network sustains itself, as well as contributes to improved medical practice and its connection to peace-building.

The CoRR program has an integrative North/South component, which goes beyond its original objective to strengthen the scientific capacity of the Southern partners. The ISLE network, established in 1995, links five Canadian universities with universities in Indonesia, the Philippines, and the Caribbean. While one of the purposes of ISLE is to strengthen island partner institutions in the South, the research 'seeks to feed back into the goals, objectives, programs and policies of sustainable development in Canada in general and specifically in Canada's island and coastal regions.'

The GURI network also tried to bridge the North-South divide through both organizational and intellectual initiatives. Thus, while the first organizational meeting of the network was held in Toronto, and attended by all prospective researchers, subsequent network-wide meetings were held successively in Cairo, Mexico City, and Washington. During the first phase of the network's operation – from 1991 through 1993 – an advisory panel consisting of four leading scholars from developing countries, one from the World Bank, and one from the United States played an active role in both the writing of papers and in the organization of meetings in all twelve subregions of the developing world. In an article on the methodology of comparative urban research, Lisa Peattie, an advisory panel member, made the important argument that distinctions between 'First' and 'Third' worlds, between 'socialist' and 'capitalist,' and between 'developed' and 'underdeveloped' were no longer useful:

> These categories seem less and less appealing as ways of slicing up the intellectual terrain. The collapse of political structures in the socialist world has uncovered issues and processes that seem quite familiar to those on the other side of the Curtain. The 'developed' versus 'underdeveloped' scheme has been breached by the identification of newly developed countries, some of them the object of envious admiration by the former leaders of the development path, and by the realization that there are different sorts of underdeveloped countries and a variety of paths to development. It has been found that it is possible for the developed world to borrow programs, like sites and services projects, from the Third World, and that phenomena first identified in the Third World have their analogues in the First World – for example, the 'informal sector.'[19]

Carrying the argument further, Michael Cohen, the director of the World Bank's Urban Development Division, proposed the hypothesis 'that cities in the North and South are becoming more alike in their most important characteristics: growing unemployment, declining infrastructure, deteriorating environment, collapsing social compact, and institutional weakness.' But he also points out that, just as these objective conditions are becoming more similar, 'their meanings are becoming more local and subjective.'[20] While Cohen was not a formal member of any GURI committee or group, from his position within the World Bank he was closely involved in and supportive of GURI's development, and invited papers from four major GURI researchers in the collaborative book in which his 'convergence' article appeared.

LEAP is yet another example of the increasing integration between Northern and Southern perspectives on development. LEAP initiated a 'green jobs' project near Kingston, Ontario, and found a donor to support it. The project is carried out by groups in the community itself, while being monitored and evaluated by OISE. As a result of its activities in communities in Canada, the Canadian role in the LEAP network is one of partnership, rather than management. When the term of the current Canadian coordinator comes to an end, it is expected that one of the Southern regions will assume the responsibility.

The Sustainability of Knowledge Networks

As we have seen, many knowledge networks that work through universities are horizontal, flexible, and relatively fluid structures. Unlike organizations that, at times, live on long past the need they were designed to serve, networks should face the obverse challenge: sustaining themselves over time. A strong knowledge network requires strong nodes, and strong nodes require infrastructure to support their work with other nodes in the network. Funding and support are important issues, even in knowledge networks. But to survive, a network must also meet the felt needs of its members. When members need to work together to solve a shared problem, the barriers to multidisciplinary and cross-cultural research seem less daunting. The needs of members must also be met in ways that are respectful of their autonomy, or members will drift away.

Funding was essential to the origins and development of all five knowledge networks discussed in this study. Substantial grants were required to start these networks. The Ford Foundation provided a start-up grant and follow-on investment of CAD $6,461,696 to GURI. The Foundation was what the project's director termed 'a dream donor.' When the original plans were being developed, he was told by the Foundation to imagine that funding was not a problem and to budget for whatever the network needed to succeed: infrastructure, support, travel, additional staff at the core, and an advisory committee. The strong infrastructure of GURI made it easier to raise additional funds. The budget for GURI in its three phases was well over $7 million. The Ford Foundation grant came to an end with completion of the third phase, and GURI would have to find additional funding if it was to continue, even at a more modest level.

CISEPO was also fortunate in its founding donor. A family foundation has provided most of the CAD $2.5 million that the network has required since its inception. The director has raised additional funds from other foundations, NGOs, and medical institutions. The annual budget is $300,000 and needs are growing as CISEPO expands its programming. The founding donor has recently reduced funding by 40 per cent, and CISEPO is now aggressively pursuing support from both the private sector and public benefactors. The fund-raising effort requires additional infrastructure, and new donors are likely to require more formal reporting than the original donor. To meet these requirements, the network will have to invest in additional support staff.

CARNET received CAD $5 million from the federal government of Canada and two granting agencies. Stringent reporting requirements were established which consumed disproportionate amounts of members' time. The director argued that the grant fell far short of what was required to sustain the network; infrastructure costs were 'real' and 'significant.'[21] Significant amounts were spent on travel so that members could meet. The director complained that he did not have sufficient administrative support for the coordination that the network required. Ultimately, network leaders decided not to reapply for a second round of funding because of the rigid reporting requirements and the inadequate funding.

CoRR (and ISLE) are funded by IDRC. The initial three-year funding level of CAD $300,000 per year was extended at a yearly level of $115,000 to cover salaries of the administrative staff and project activities. IDRC has proven to be a flexible and supportive funder, who has allowed network members to adjust as new opportunities arise. Members also pay $20 per subscription to the newsletter, but subscription fees are not a significant component of CoRR's budget. The network remains dependent on its principal funder.

LEAP's budget for its international activities and interregional coordination is currently CAD $110,000 per year, double its initial budget. It receives its funds from CIDA and the Swedish agency SIDA; funding is renewable every three years. Additional funds for specific programs are raised from public agencies and the private sector. Regional coordinators receive a small sum from the central office yearly to develop their networks, and are also encouraged to do their own fund-raising. Although the funding from Sweden and Canada is reasonably stable, and LEAP receives a high level of support from a well-established international institution (ICAE), the coordinator nevertheless spends one-third of her time on fund-raising.

The pattern is clear: knowledge networks require sizeable and stable funding in order to develop the infrastructure that is essential to support research and dissemination, and to fund the travel and meetings that are required even when electronic communication is accessible. The funding should be stable, but flexible, so that network members can take advantage of the flexibility they have and change course as new opportunities arise. Reporting requirements must also be flexible, so that already overburdened network members are not 'buried' in bureaucratic processes which interfere with their capacity to do the work; this was the story of CARNET. In all five cases, the dollar amounts do not capture a significant part of the real costs of creating and maintaining the network, in part because of the infrastructure that is contributed virtually gratis by host universities, research institutes, and hospitals, and in large part because of the extraordinary amounts of unpaid time committed voluntarily by the directors. Sizeable, stable funding, paradoxically, is often more difficult for networks to obtain than it is for hierarchical organizations with established infrastructures. Precisely because networks tend to be more flexible and more fluid in their organization, funders tend to impose more, rather than less, stringent requirements even as they seek to support the flexibility that knowledge networks can bring.

A second important requirement for a sustainable knowledge network is a strong commitment to a shared goal or the felt need to solve a common problem. LEAP members feel that they are making a special contribution to the theory and practice of adult environmental education and, consequently, have a strong commitment to the network. 'This network works better than others I have been involved in,' one coordinator commented, 'because people see the need for it, and are prepared to put time and energy into making it work.'[22] LEAP is also the most horizontally organized of the networks, with autonomous organizations in various regions which are each engaged in ongoing work. Within the relatively loose structure of the network, there is space for organizations to become more or less involved at different times, without compromising the overall health of the network. If LEAP continues to receive its funding from Canada and Sweden, it is likely to grow over time.

CISEPO is also likely to grow. Much of its programming meets the fundamental needs that its partners define. The medical services, as well as the knowledge that the network provides, are desperately needed, and in many cases the services cannot be provided without members working together. Sustained, flexible funding combined with flexible management also has enabled the network to adapt readily in a fluid, shifting environment and to embrace opportunities that this environment provides.

The same factors explain CoRR's success in sustaining itself and in spinning off a new network to meet new challenges. As with CISEPO and LEAP, sustained funding enabled relatively effective coordination and administration of the network. As the network grew and the workload increased, the coordinator was able to add a research associate to the team. The network grew because the problem it addressed is important to the members, and the way the problem is addressed reflects their needs and concerns.

One of the networks, CARNET, decided not to renew itself, largely but not exclusively because of the onerous requirements of the funder. Cross-disciplinary work between interested communities is challenging at best: researchers need to share an overarching problem. CARNET, one of the research directors maintained, was a network of experts conducting research on aging but without a common research problem that demanded collaborative efforts. As the benefits were not cross-disciplinary but remained essentially within each group, there was little incentive to maintain the network in the face of onerous reporting requirements.

The future of GURI, one of the strongest networks, is also problematic. In spite of the network's success during the 1990s, it is extremely unlikely that GURI will continue to operate in more than a purely informal fashion now that the Ford Foundation's third and final phase of funding has ended and the coordinator's responsibilities have formally been terminated. GURI was not sustainable globally without further funding from a major donor – though several of the subregional networks might continue to function. The low level of communication at the regional and subregional levels suggests that the network will probably not continue to function formally at these levels. The members of the network in different regions belong to different academic disciplines and may not have sufficient reason to consult each other in the absence of an active project, with tangible, precise objectives. Further, the regional nodes have not, by and large, succeeded in establishing vital links between subregions. As one of the researchers notes, 'one of the most problematic elements, in my opinion, has been maintaining a good system of communication between the different groups in the subregions, and above all between the researchers in the different regions, such that when the project and the coordination from the core ends, the network could continue in the developing world.'[23] Without a well-funded, highly organized, and interesting collaborative research project, there may be little motivation to continue the networking process.

Whether a network sustains itself over time is an appropriate criterion of evaluation only if the problem the network was designed to address initially is still important to the members. One of the advantages of networks, unlike more hierarchically organized institutions, is their capacity to disappear or reconstruct themselves in new ways to meet new problems. GURI, for example, was created to facilitate a finite research project, not to become a sustainable network over time. Nevertheless, it is difficult to imagine that we know all we need to know about urban governance, or that there are not other pressing urban issues common to network members. The critical obstacle GURI faced was sustainable funding at a high enough level to provide the support and infrastructure, as well as focus, that had been central to the network's success.

Conclusion

Four of the five cases considered in this study – all of them examples of university-connected, knowledge-based networks – have made important contributions both in their own substantive areas, and in improving concepts of development. While they had limitations of resources, of commitment, of continuity in the face of fluctuating involvement of groups and individuals, or of organization, they were able to transcend most of these limitations and set a pattern for a new approach to collaborative work. Indeed, the potential of these kinds of networks for constructive and sustainable collaboration over long periods of time with relatively minimal resources is so great that this organizational form has become the dominant modality in development research.

Universities can do a lot more to develop and sustain these networks. But to facilitate their supportive role, they must themselves receive greater reinforcement both from their traditional supporters – governments and the private sector – and from the community of scholars and researchers whose professional purview does not yet fully incorporate interdisciplinary, operational project work as a 'normal' academic activity.

Universities in the North have colleagues and partners in universities in the South. During the 1970s and 1980s, universities in a great number of Southern countries were ravaged by national governments whose shrinking budgets and increasing debt loads did not permit them to adequately fund higher education; by political regimes who saw in universities the seeds of both current and future opposition to their policies; and by other countries and opportunity structures that drew away some of their most knowledgeable and talented researchers for better facilities and higher salaries. Until recently, Southern universities have been a virtually forgotten institution in official development assistance, as programs to develop infrastructure, to develop and maintain basic community health and primary education, and to reform governmental and parastatal institutions have taken pride of place. While a great many needs require response, important knowledge institutions like universities, where the training of both the technicians and the future leaders takes place, must find new sources of support. Networks based in Northern academic institutions will be much more effective and sustainable if their partners in the South have better libraries, better conditions of work, and better information technology. At present, the rapid polarization of informational infrastructure – satellite technology, telephone connections, and even basic computer availability – between poor and wealthy countries threatens to isolate poor regions of the world – especially Africa – from the benefits of the kinds of network we have been describing. While some donors, such as IDRC, have been acutely aware of this problem and have tried to address it,[24] the level of investment to bring developing countries up to the standards of the North in terms of information technology and infrastructure is too massive for any single agency – or even a group of agencies – to deal with effectively.

Simply strengthening universities as institutions will not be a sufficient basis for nurturing knowledge networks – in both the North and the South. One of the central characteristics of these networks is their interdisciplinarity. Because networks are open to the needs of a diverse membership, because they respond very often to real-life challenges in local communities, and because they incorporate both university researchers and NGOs – and even governmental members – they operate on the fringes of the internationally established academic disciplines in whose cultures most of their members have originally been trained. But while interdisciplinarity is a strength, it is also a weakness in many situations. Interdisciplinary programs and facilities at universities are often the poor cousins of major departmental programs that are based essentially on the classical disciplines that have been built up incrementally since the nineteenth century in both Europe and North America. None of the networks in our study had its organizational base in a conventional academic department, even though many of their members spent much of their time as disciplinary specialists. In his Canadian study of scientific knowledge networks, Howard Clark suggests that

> the university over the last five decades has become less and less a community. Faculty members and researchers feel far more involved and committed to their discipline and even a sub-discipline than to the university as an institution. The university becomes more and more the landlord who provides buildings and other facilities such as computers, scientific equipment and a library, as well as accounting services for research funds; but it is not the intellectual community to which the faculty members give first allegiance.[25]

This generalization seems overstated. While disciplinary homes predominate, our cases demonstrate that universities are increasingly active in supporting innovative, cross-community, interdisciplinary research. To strengthen interdisciplinary studies – at least in the area of development – universities will want to continue to encourage partnerships and collegial relationships with NGOs and private sector groups, and to encourage their students through cooperative learning and exchange relationships with institutions in the South. As they do this, universities will, perforce, operate more like knowledge-based networks themselves.

Finally, how can granting agencies and donor organizations support this process? First, they must encourage detailed studies of networks, far more extensive than this 'first cut,' in many fields. In recent years, some major international institutions have attempted to develop their own expertise on the 'knowledge' side of knowledge-based networks, and have partnered with developing-country researchers and institutions to pursue thematic-based programs. We need to know more about how interdisciplinary knowledge-based networks operate, who their partners are, what are their strengths and weaknesses, and how they differ from more traditional disciplinary knowledge production.

Second, agency-based initiatives, more often than not, include Northern researchers as individuals but not in their institutional representation; the same is generally true for the Southern researchers. But if these networks do not recognize the indispensable role of universities, both in the North and in the South, in the training of future researchers, and in the dissemination of knowledge in their own countries – a recognition that can take place through support of administrative and indirect costs in the institutions through project funding – the contributions of networks will be short-term. Universities, agencies, NGOs, and the private sector can work together profitably, but we need to establish protocols such that individual partners – whether these are the agencies themselves, or the universities, or the NGOs – are adequately supported and can carry out appropriate roles within complex partnerships. It is important to establish these protocols so that there is a constructive and positive arrangement among and between the various partners. Currently, the major strengths of universities, and university centres and institutes, lie in teaching and long-term training, and in research and writing; that of NGOs in community mobilization and involvement of the energies and commitment of volunteer activists; that of the private sector, including businesses and consultants, in the efficient organization of projects and of focused technical work in specific areas; and of donor agencies in mobilizing funding at the national and international levels, in designing and managing large-scale programs of assistance and research, and in connecting Northern interests with Southern needs. For networks to function effectively, the partners ought to contribute from strength, and to receive according to their institutional needs.

Finally, we need to develop mechanisms for more flexible, and longer-term funding for networks. Networks may expand and contract over time, and they may change their key personnel and even their central objectives. But if they have merit and are contributing to the expansion of knowledge and improved practice, they should not have to be constantly preoccupied, even obsessed, with continuity in funding. To some extent, this is a minor problem insofar as the network principle is itself a response to achieve organizational flexibility in the face of uncertain resources and support. But the complexity of networks also makes funding more problematic in the sense that donor agencies and funding sources are not yet themselves organized to respond to their emerging needs. And when they do respond to the network imperative, donors often 'see and use networks as mechanisms through which to foster their own agendas; to produce specific goals within specific schedules and budgets.'[26] If they are to support networks in a truly facilitative fashion, donors must refine their policies so that they can encourage network friendly programs, even if this involves more networking with other donors and funding agencies in order to achieve a better fit. As our case studies have illustrated, funding makes a big difference to outcomes; providing outputs are of high quality, long-term funding needs to be found so that this innovative approach to knowledge production and application can reach its full potential.

NOTES

1 Manuel Castells, *The Power of Identity*, vol. 2 of *The Information Age* (Oxford: Blackwell, 1997), 254. The degree to which the nation-state has lost power because of political choice or forces outside its control is a matter of heated debate. For arguments that states have chosen to accept a more dependent role in certain functional areas, see, for example, Eric Helleiner, *States and the Reemergence of Global Finance: From Bretton Woods to the 1990s* (Ithaca: Cornell University Press, 1994); Paul Hirst and Grahame Thompson, *Globalization in Question: The International Economy and the Possibilities of Governance* (Cambridge: Polity Press, 1996); and Linda McQuaig, *The Cult of Impotence: Selling the Myth of Powerlessness in the Global Economy* (Toronto: Viking, 1998).
2 Neil Nevitte, *The Decline of Deference* (Peterborough, ON: Broadview, 1996); Joseph S. Nye, Philip D. Zelikow, and David C. King, *Why People Don't Trust Government* (Cambridge, MA: Harvard University Press, 1997).
3 Robert D. Putnam, Susan J. Pharr, and Russell J. Dalton, 'Introduction: What's Troubling the Trilateral Democracies?' in *Disaffected Democracies: What's Troubling the Trilateral Countries?* ed. Susan J. Pharr and Robert D. Putnam (Princeton: Princeton University Press, 2000), 21.
4 In 1997 a poll reported in the *Washington Post* showed a public confidence

rate of only 22 per cent in federal institutions, as against 38 per cent in those at the local level. See Nye, Zelikow, and King, eds, *Why People Don't Trust Government*, 1.

5 Ronald Inglehart, 'Postmaterialist Values and the Erosion of Institutional Authority,' in Nye, Zelikow, and King, eds, *Why People Don't Trust Government*, 217–36.

6 Arturo Escobar, *Encountering Development: The Making and Unmaking of the Third World* (Princeton: Princeton University Press, 1996), esp. chapter 6.

7 This critique is somewhat muted by now, given the cutbacks that the United Nations and Northern assistance agencies suffered during the 1990s. But the most provocative, and widely read, statement of the case against the immorality of Northern aid agencies was the book by Graham Hancock, *Lords of Poverty: The Power, Prestige, and Corruption of the International Aid Business* (London: Macmillan, 1989).

8 Robert Chambers, *Whose Reality Counts? Putting the First Last* (London: Intermediate Technology Publications, 1997).

9 Ibid., chap. 10.

10 John Naisbitt, *Megatrends Asia: Eight Asian Megatrends That Are Reshaping Our World* (New York: Simon and Schuster, 1996), 231.

11 Gustav Ranis, 'The World Bank near the Turn of the Century,' in *Global Development Fifty Years after Bretton Woods: Essays in Honour of Gerald K. Helleiner*, ed. Roy Culpeper, Albert Berry, and Frances Stewart (London: Macmillan, 1997), 78.

12 Michael H.K. Irwin, 'Banking on Poverty: An Insider's Look at the World Bank,' in *Fifty Years Is Enough: The Case against the World Bank and the International Monetary Fund*, ed. Kevin Danaher (Boston: South End Press, 1994), 153.

13 Susan George and Fabrizio Sabelli, *Faith and Credit: The World Bank's Secular Empire* (Boulder: Westview, 1994), chap. 10. In this book, the Bank is depicted as a 'supranational, non-democratic institution [which] functions very much like the Church, in fact the medieval Church. It has a doctrine, a rigidly structured hierarchy preaching and imposing this doctrine and a quasi-religious mode of self-justification' (p. 5).

14 James D. Wolfensohn, 'The World Bank and the Evolving Challenges of Development' (speech given in Washington, DC, 16 May 1997; available on the internet from the World Bank's home page: www.worldbank.org).

15 'The World Bank: A Study of Donor Nations' Perceptions: Summary Report' (unpublished document supplied by Applied Research and Consulting LLC, November 1998), p. 20.

16 Ibid.

17 World Bank, *World Development Report 1998: Knowledge for Development* (Washington, DC: World Bank, 1998), 133.

18 Ibid., 137.

19 Lisa Peattie, 'Urban Research in the 1990s,' in *Preparing for the Urban Future: Global Pressures and Local Forces*, ed. Michael A. Cohen et al. (Washington, DC: Woodrow Wilson Center Press, 1996), 398.

20 Michael Cohen, 'The Hypothesis of Urban Convergence: Are Cities in the North and South Becoming More Alike in an Age of Globalization?' in Cohen et al., eds, *Preparing for the Urban Future*, 25, 36.

21 Interview, Dr Victor Marshall, 15 August 1997.

22 Interview, Kerrie Strathy, 6 October 1997.

23 Interview, Martha Schteingart, 21 July 1997.

24 For example, to both extend its own connectivity to the projects it supported, and to facilitate better collaboration among Third World researchers, in the late 1990s IDRC developed a program – called Uganisha – that effectively subsidized some combination of technical advice, training, and internet and e-mail access for some 181 projects. IDRC's own evaluation of Uganisha indicates that it was very successful.

25 Howard C. Clark, *Formal Knowledge Networks: A Study of Canadian Experiences* (Winnipeg: International Institute of Sustainable Development, 1998), 31.

26 Anne K. Bernard, 'IDRC Networks: An Ethnographic Perspective' (IDRC Evaluation Unit, Ottawa, September 1996), 34.

Appendix A
Template Questions

I. Introduction

- A brief overview of the network.
- Historical development (formation and change).

Formation
1. Why was this network created? Why was it created in this way?
2. How was it created?
3. How long did the process take for the network to become established?
4. What personal links or contacts informed the creation of the network?
5. What was the economic or social context that made the network necessary?
6. What analysis or forces informed the decision to create the network? For example, was it a top-down initiative in response to a particular problem or was it from the bottom up?

II. Objectives

- Mission and goals.

III. Governance

- Structure and organization of the network.

- Decision-making and coordination.
- Membership.
- Communication between members.
- Evaluation of products, processes, and strategic development.

Organizational Structure
1. Who are the members of your network? Institutions, individuals, or both? In theory? In practice?
2. How long do they remain active? Is membership stable or fluid?
3. What are the criteria for membership? Is it open or exclusive? Is there a contract that outlines the obligations of membership?
4. How do you make decisions in the network? Is the network hierarchical, consensual, or a combination? Is the process horizontal (across network members) or vertical (centralized)?
5. How involved are your members in the network activities? Please provide some specific examples.
6. How is your agenda coordinated? Who sets it?
7. Who controls the funds? Who manages the progress reporting?

Membership and Communication
1. How frequently do your members meet or interact? Formally and informally?
2. What is the nature of their interaction?
3. Are members constrained or open in the information that they exchange? Is the network a force for solidarity?

Evaluation
1. What mechanisms do you use to evaluate the effectiveness of the network in meeting its objectives?
2. What are the criteria for success?
3. Is there a relationship between funding and evaluation?
4. What factors most contribute to the success of the network?
5. What factors are the most problematic for the network?

IV. Products and Activities

- Tangible products (e.g., research papers) and processes (e.g., relationship-building, conferences).
- Policy action.

Products
1. What is the overarching product/project of the network? Does it produce tangible products?
2. How and to whom are the knowledge and tangible products created and transmitted? Is the network a collaborative project between network members only? How/through what means do they collaborate?
3. If the network member would have produced the product or knowledge anyway, how did the network add value to the result?

V. Funding

- Profile and role of grantors.
- Conditions of grants.
- Funding requirements and patterns.
- Investment required by coordinator and administrative staff.

1. How many funders support your network?
2. Who are they?
3. How much support do they provide (please provide specific figures)? Did they give a one-time gift or do they provide ongoing support to sustain the network? If ongoing, what is the payment schedule (annually, quarterly, dependent upon financial and research progress reports)?
4. On what basis are the grants made? What are the obligations you must adhere to?
5. How much are you paid to work on this network? Is the money provided through the grantors or do you donate your time from other projects?
6. How much time per week do you put into this network?
7. Do the grantors play a nurturing role or a fragmenting role?
8. How has the funding changed over time?
9. How, if at all, does the funder's agenda determine the network's?
10. How flexible are the funders in reporting requirements, contractual changes, etc.?

VI. Impacts and Benefits

Capacity-Building and Policy Action
1. Is the capacity to contribute to policy discussion strengthened as a result of network activities? How?
2. How are people improved (researchers / scientists / teachers / graduate students / government and policy officials)?
3. Do members receive access to contacts and information that they otherwise would not see or know about as a result of network activities?
4. Please provide some concrete examples of success of the network. For example, how has your network created institutional capacity?

Feedback
1. How do the network's activities feed back into Canadian needs and issues?
2. How do the network's activities feed back into locations in which it operates?

'Higher Order Knowledge' and Operational Knowledge
1. What kind of knowledge is transmitted? What makes this knowledge unique and dependent upon the network for its creation? That is, how do you know that this product or knowledge would not be produced without the network?
2. Does the knowledge connect conceptual and operational?

VII. Sustainability

Sustaining the Network: Change and Reform
1. How do you build and maintain the network? How has it changed over time and what led to these changes?
2. What mechanisms do you use to sustain and develop the network (i.e., electronic communications / conferences / coordination with other networks)?
3. What is the role of the Executive Director in the process of network development?
4. How frequently do you use electronic communications to sustain the network?
5. What is the role of universities and government in sustaining networks, based on your experience?

COMPARATIVE ANALYSIS TEMPLATE QUESTIONS

1. What criteria do we use to evaluate the effectiveness of a network?
2. Under what conditions are networks most effective? When are they ineffective? In other words, what are the combination of variables that positively reinforce each other to produce a successful network? How do the variables interact; that is, are there trade-offs between variables?
3. What are the lessons learned – comparatively (e.g., what can CoRR learn from GURI, etc.)?
4. What do we mean by higher order knowledge?
5. Under what conditions do networks produce this higher order knowledge?
6. How does this knowledge impact outcomes of a network, that is, improve the quality of policies and programs?
7. What kind of networks are our cases and what difference does that make for how they work, that is, joint production of knowledge/collaboration for the delivery of services?
8. How do we know networks make a difference?
9. We know networks are not low maintenance. What does it take to sustain them?
10. How does the governance (democratic leadership) of the network impact its efficiency and its effectiveness (i.e., steering committee composition, decision process, is there a trade-off between efficiency and effectiveness)?
11. How do efficiency and funding interact? Does money allow for communication?
12. How does funding determine organizational structure (i.e., you generally need money for a decentralized network; some funders will not allow a decentralized network)?
13. What type of hub is needed? How does funding determine the nature of the hub? For example, healthy hubs require healthy funding. If you want to have a Canadian hub, you will need Canadian funding.

Appendix B
Comparative Characteristics
of the Five Networks

Appendix B

Comparative Characteristics of the Five Networks

CARNET	CISEPO	CoRR/ISLE	GURI	LEAP	Comparative Issues
Objectives • Produce research useful to entrepreneurs and citizens on social implications of aging population • Establish partnerships between industry and academic community • Provide research opportunities for young academics	**Objectives** • Use scientific collaboration to promote peace-building in regions of conflict • Foster collaborative medical research and education across borders and disciplines	**Objectives** • Provide coordination and support for IDRC coastal projects • Facilitate interaction among projects and researchers and others, especially between natural and social scientists • Assist work with coastal communities to improve quality of life through sustainable management of living coastal aquatic resources	**Objectives** • Produce research that contributes to better understanding of Third World urban issues to inform urban policies • Strengthen professional skills and institutional position of local researchers in Third World • Influence Ford Foundation's regional offices to integrate urban concerns into their work	**Objectives** • Develop theories and strategies for environmental adult education • Raise awareness of environmental issues in adult education • Help environmental groups strengthen education work through adult education perspective • Strengthen links between community and academic knowledge	**Objectives** • Except GURI, each network has objectives related to promoting interaction between groups that might not otherwise interact – business and academia in CARNET's case; representatives from 'opposing' sides in conflict areas in CISEPO's case; natural and social scientists in CoRR's case; community and academic knowledge-producers in LEAP's case; and, in practice, interaction is facilitated through GURI bringing together academics from different geographical areas. • CARNET and GURI objectives are most product-oriented; others emphasize networking process as part of the product.

Appendix B—(*continued*)
Comparative Characteristics of the Five Networks

CARNET	CISEPO	CoRR/ISLE	GURI	LEAP	Comparative Issues
Governance *Coordination:* • Governed by tri-council directorate of funders and advised by steering committee of representatives from member universities, partner corporations, research institutes, and government • Day-to-day management by research directors, advised by business representatives • Central coordinating unit at University of Toronto	**Governance** *Coordination:* • Governed by director with board that includes key funder, community representatives, and scientists • Coordinator influences direction of major projects and fosters support for the network, but operates with consensual style; team members given high degree of freedom and flexibility in direction and implementation of projects • Loosely structured, less centralized	**Governance** *Coordination:* • Coordinator directly accountable to funder • Most coordination and networking related to coordinator's yearly visits to projects • Relatively structured, relatively centralized	**Governance** *Coordination:* • Relatively tight central administrative control • Consensus-oriented; trust is key • Personality of coordinator facilitates networking. • Reputation and contacts of coordinator are significant motivation for members' involvement. • Directions set in full network meetings, with guidance from coordinators and some input from funders • Small core membership of twelve regional/subregional coordinators, who develop own networks at local level • Highly structured, semi-decentralized	**Governance** *Coordination:* • Consensus-oriented; trust is key • Coordinator is accountable to members but has freedom to take initiatives. • Coordinator's job not permanent; position rotates among regions • Network a program of parent organization (ICAE) • Directions for network set in consultation with members in interregional meetings • Semi-structured, quite decentralized (regions operate with high degree of autonomy)	**Governance** *Coordination:* • CARNET is the most structured network, with the most direct funder involvement in governance; LEAP is the most decentralized, with the most autonomous network nodes. • Personality and leadership of central coordinator plays crucial roles in all the networks; status, contacts, and personality of coordinator seem somewhat less important in LEAP than in CISEPO, CoRR, and GURI. • Decision-making is informal in all, and consensus, or at least consultation, is favoured. • Administrative and logistical tasks are largely centralized in all the networks.

Appendix B—(continued)

Comparative Characteristics of the Five Networks

CARNET	CISEPO	CoRR/ISLE	GURI	LEAP	Comparative Issues
Membership: • Researchers across disciplines from ten universities and one consulting firm	*Membership:* • Leading researchers in medical fields and partner health organizations around the world • Shared commitment to peace-building	*Membership:* • Leading natural and social scientists in the South and North who address research on resources of coastal communities • Includes members from ten IDRC projects	*Membership:* • Diverse membership in terms of culture, geography, academic discipline, gender, age, and status • Solidarity arising from shared belief that urban issues are important but relatively marginalized • Shared intellectual engagement in innovative research	*Membership:* • 1,500 people/orgnizations that receive newsletter • Each region represented by organizational delegate who acts as regional coordinator • Solidarity arising from shared commitment to environmental adult education and sense this area is marginalized	*Membership:* • Membership is diverse in various ways in all networks (except CARNET, in which all members are academics, and business contacts are characterized as partners of, rather than members in, the network). • All networks have a core group (e.g., subregional and regional coordinators in GURI, regional representatives in LEAP), with an extended network based on involvement in network or local subnetworks based on involvement in network activities, receipt of newsletter, etc.
Communication: • Members communicate via scheduled colloquia, meetings, and research sessions. • Communication by newsletter, fax, and e-mail secondary to face-to-face meetings • Highly structured and centralized	*Communication:* • Centred first around the coordinating unit in Toronto, and then ad hoc between regional members outside Toronto's facilitative role • Primarily via fax, phone, and, more recently, e-mail; face-to-face meetings through continuing edu-	*Communication:* • Regular newsletter keeps members informed and connected. • In 1989, 150 received newsletter; now 700. • Everyone on newsletter mailing list is considered a member of CoRR, but primary network members are directly connected to	*Communication:* • Regular communication within subregional networks; less between regions except in face-to-face meetings	*Communication:* • Meetings, and via newsletter and e-mail • Problems with communication and network development in some regions	*Communication:* • Face-to-face communication is an important supplement to, or more important than, other forms (e-mail, etc.) in all networks.

Comparative Characteristics of the Five Networks

CARNET	CISEPO	CoRR/ISLE	GURI	LEAP	Comparative Issues
	Communication: (concluded) cation workshops are critical	*Communication:* (concluded) the projects as well. • Uncertain whether, or how much, members communicate directly with each other outside major meetings or summer institute at Dalhousie			
Evaluation: • Information assembled by the tri-council directorate facilitates assessment of products and outputs. The process – which is frequently one of interaction between network members – is measured.	*Evaluation:* • No systematic evaluation conducted on the impact of the network's scientific activities on regional peace-building • Occasional evaluation after network events and on clinical interventions	*Evaluation:* • No evaluation conducted by the network director	*Evaluation:* • No evaluation conducted by network or funder	*Evaluation:* • No systematic evaluation mechanism	*Evaluation:* • Evaluation is sparse to non-existent in all networks.
Products and Activities • Lectures, papers, articles, chapters of books, and complete books focused on aging in individual, work, and family contexts; identification and provision of related products and services • Highly product-oriented	**Products and Activities** • Scientific exchanges; visiting professor program; joint educational and clinical programs such as research prizes, continuing education programs, international scientific meetings, and graduate training/education • Activities involve collaboration between people from	**Products and Activities** • Workshops, working group meetings, annual summer institutes • Research exchanges • Newsletter • Coordinators provide research support, such as literature searches, to project leaders. • Publications from workshops and exchanges	**Products and Activities** • Articles and books • Subregional, regional, and global meetings involving researchers, policy-makers, NGO representatives, and donors • Research process involving academics, community leaders, policy-makers (especially in Phase 3) • Product-oriented, but	**Products and Activities** • Involved in many diverse activities: community projects, research, study circles, publication, attending international meetings, academic conferences • Some activities carried out as LEAP; others facilitated by LEAP but carried out by other organizations • LEAP role to give inter-	**Products and Activities** • All networks have identifiable products or outcomes that are in some way tangible (books, meetings, projects, etc.). • Process and product are closely linked in all the networks, but emphasis varies: LEAP's purpose is *to network*;

Appendix B—(continued)

Comparative Characteristics of the Five Networks

CARNET	CISEPO	CoRR/ISLE	GURI	LEAP	Comparative Issues
	Products and Activities (concluded) • regions in conflict (e.g., Israeli-Palestinian-Jordanian collaboration). Many articles result from collaboration. • Research production processes designed to contribute to peace-building • Capacity-building strong	**Products and Activities (concluded)** • (though not directly attributed to the network) • Oriented to networking and research facilitation • Assisted in creation of new ISLE network	**Products and Activities (concluded)** • network-building valued highly	**Products and Activities (concluded)** • national profile to experiences and lessons derived from projects; and to facilitate networking. • Product and process equally important	**Products and Activities (concluded)** GURI and CARNET are both projects organized as networks (i.e., the network is a means to an end); CoRR could be termed a network *made up of* projects; CISEPO's networking facilitates scientific collaboration but is also part of the process of peace-building.
Funding • Some suggestions it was insufficient, but funds provided were high among the networks • Reporting requirements too complex and not tied to project goals • Donor agenda-setting • Researchers applied for funding. • Coordinated funding through three major donors	**Funding** • Generous and supportive donor • Collaborative relationship with donor • Funder sits on board of directors. • Coordinator approached donor. • One major core donor, with a few others, including patients • Funding shifting to broader donor base	**Funding** • Sufficient funding • Program-style • Original idea from donor • One donor	**Funding** • Generous, supportive primary donor • Collaborative relationship with primary donor • Funding provides professional opportunities to resource-poor researchers in developing countires. • Program-style • Original idea from donor • One major core donor plus some others funding specific aspects of network	**Funding** • Program-style • Major donor believes in goals of network. • Network approached donors. • Portion of core funding allocated by parent organization (ICAE) • Coordinator works at least double her paid hours. • Two core donors plus numerous funding sources for individual projects • Central coordinator	**Funding** • All networks have at least core funding that is stable over relatively long periods (i.e., program-style or multi-year funding). • CoRR and GURI were donor-initiated, but especially with GURI, control over the network has since been primarily in network hands; CISEPO and LEAP were network-initiated; in CARNET,

Appendix B—*(continued)*
Comparative Characteristics of the Five Networks

CARNET	CISEPO	CoRR/ISLE	GURI	LEAP	Comparative Issues
				Funding *(concluded)* spends about one-third of time on funding-related activities.	**Funding** *(concluded)* researchers applied to donor but through a pre-existing program. • GURI stands out for having particularly generous funding; LEAP stands out for having the tightest funding situation (highly dependent on the willingness of central coordinator to donate time); also, LEAP has only core funding but must engage in on-going fund-raising for network projects. • All networks have only one, or one major or dominant, donor (CARNET has three, but these channel funds through the same structured program; CISEPO is broadening its donor base). • CoRR is satisfied with funding levels; CISEPO is seeking to expand donor base, as is LEAP.

Appendix B—*(concluded)*
Comparative Characteristics of the Five Networks

CARNET	CISEPO	CoRR/ISLE	GURI	LEAP	Comparative Issues
Impacts and Benefits • Good link between conceptual and operational • Brought parties together within disciplines that were not previously communicating • Trained and supported graduate students	**Impacts and Benefits** • Capacity-building for researchers, scientists, practitioners, and students • Cultivates and sustains relationships among professionals that otherwise would not occur • Pursues social, economic, and political goals through medical research • Good link between conceptual and operational	**Impacts and Benefits** • Links scientific research to local needs and conditions • Capacity-building for local researchers and project leaders • Promotes South/South exchange	**Impacts and Benefits** • Increases capacity of researchers to influence and participate in policy-making • Raises profile of urban issues • Increased communication among urban researchers within subregions and, to lesser extent, between regions	**Impacts and Benefits** • Provides support for people working in field • Bridges academic and on-the-ground knowledge and experiences • Facilitates access to funds for organizations working on environmental adult education in South • Opens access to policy-makers on environmental adult education issues • Facilitates South/South links	**Impacts and Benefits** • CARNET, CISEPO, CoRR, and LEAP: strong link between conceptual and operational • CoRR and LEAP: strong connection between interdisciplinary researchers • GURI, CARNET, and CISEPO: strong link between students and senior scholars • GURI enhances capacity of researchers to participate in policy-making. • LEAP and CISEPO seek to change the frameworks around which policies are made and evaluated. • CISEPO, LEAP, and CoRR promote capacity-building through training, and/or education.

Bibliography

Adler, Emmanuel. 'The Emergence of Cooperation: National Epistemic
Communities and the International Evolution of the Idea of Arms Control.'
International Organization 46 (Winter 1992): 101–46.

Annan, Kofi. *Program for U.N. Reform.* New York: United Nations, July
1997.

Applied Research and Consulting LLC. 'The World Bank: A Study of Donor
Nations' Perceptions: Summary Report.' Unpublished document supplied
by Applied Research and Consulting LLC, November 1998.

Argyris, Chris, and Donald A. Schon. *Organizational Learning: A Theory of
Action Perspective.* Boston: Addison-Wesley, 1978.

– *Strategy, Change and Defensive Routines.* Boston: Pitman, 1985.

Atkinson, Michael M., and William D. Coleman. 'Policy Networks, Policy
Communities, and the Problems of Governance.' In *Policy Studies in Canada:
The State of the Art,* ed. Laurent Dobuzinskis, Michael Howlett, and David
Laycock, 193–218. Toronto: University of Toronto Press, 1996.

Barzelay, Michael. *Breaking through Bureaucracy.* Berkeley: University of
California Press, 1992.

Bernard, Anne K. 'IDRC Networks: An Ethnographic Perspective.' IDRC
Evaluation Unit, Ottawa, September 1996.

Bohm, David, ed. *Thought as a System.* London: Routledge, 1994.

Bourdieu, Pierre. *Distinction.* Trans. Richard Nice. London: Routledge and
Kegan Paul, 1984.

– *Homo Academicus* Stanford: Stanford University Press, 1988.

CARNET. *Into the Age of Aging: Selected Findings.* Toronto: Institute for Human
Development, Life Course, and Aging, University of Toronto, 1996.

Castells, Manuel. *The Rise of the Network Society.* Vol. 1 of *The Information Age:
Economy, Society and Culture.* Oxford: Blackwell, 1996.

– *The Power of Identity.* Vol. 2 of *The Information Age: Economy, Society and Culture.* Oxford: Blackwell, 1997.

Chambers, Robert. *Whose Reality Counts? Putting the First Last.* London: ntermediate Technology Publications, 1997.

Chawla, Sarita, and John Renesch, eds. *Learning Organizations: Developing Cultures for Tomorrow's Workplace.* Portland: Productivity Press, 1995.

Checkel, Jeffrey T. 'Ideas, Institutions, and the Gorbachev Foreign Policy Revolution.' *World Politics* 45 (Jan. 1993): 242–70.

– *Ideas and International Political Change: Soviet-Russian Behavior and the End of the Cold War.* New Haven: Yale University Press, 1997.

Chichilnisky, Graciela. 'The Knowledge Revolution.' *Journal of International Trade and Economic Development* 7 (March 1998): 39–45.

Choucri, Nazli, and Steven R.L.Millman. *Knowledge Networks.* Cambridge, MA: MIT Technology and Development Program, 1998.

Clark, Howard C. *Formal Knowledge Networks: A Study of Canadian Experiences.* Winnipeg: International Institute for Sustainable Development, 1998.

Cohen, Michael. 'The Hypothesis of Urban Convergence: Are Cities in the North and South Becoming More Alike in an Age of Globalization?' In *Preparing for the Urban Future: Global Pressures and Local Forces,* ed. Michael A. Cohen, Blair A. Ruble, Joseph S. Tulchin, and Allison M. Garland, 25–38. Washington, DC: Woodrow Wilson Center Press (distributed by Johns Hopkins University Press), 1996.

Cole, Philip, Renato Roithmann, Yehudah Roth, and J.S. Chapnik. 'Measures of Airway Patency for Users of the Toronto Systems and Others Interested in Nasal Patency Measurement.' *Annals of Otology, Rhinology, and Laryngology* 106, no. 10 (Oct. 1997): 2–5.

Coleman, James S. 'Social Capital in the Creation of Human Capital.' *American Journal of Sociology* [Supplement] 94 (1988): S95–120.

– *The Foundations of Social Theory.* Cambridge: Cambridge University Press, 1990.

Collier, Paul. *Social Capital and Poverty.* Social Capital Initiative Working Paper 4. Washington, DC: World Bank, 1998.

Escobar, Arturo. *Encountering Development: The Making and Unmaking of the Third World.* Princeton: Princeton University Press, 1996.

Evangelista, Matthew. *Unarmed Forces: The Transnational Movement to End the Cold War.* Ithaca: Cornell University Press, 1999.

Flyvbjerg, Bent. *Rationality and Power: Democracy in Practice.* Chicago: University of Chicago Press, 1998.

Fukuyama, Francis. *Trust: The Social Virtues and the Creation of Prosperity.* New York: Free Press, 1995.

George, Susan, and Fabrizio Sabelli. *Faith and Credit: The World Bank's Secular Empire*. Boulder: Westview, 1994.

Gibbons, Michael, et al. *New Production of Knowledge: Dynamics of Science and Research in Contemporary Societies*. London: Sage, 1994.

Goleman, Daniel. *Working with Emotional Intelligence*. New York: Bantam Books, 1998.

Gross Stein, Janice. 'Political Learning by Doing: Gorbachev as Uncommitted Thinker and Motivated Learner.' *International Organization* 48 (Spring 1994): 155–83.

Haas, Ernest. *When Knowledge Is Power*. Berkeley: University of California Press, 1990.

Haas, Peter M. 'Introduction: Epistemic Communities and International Policy Coordination.' In special issue on 'Knowledge, Power, and International Policy Coordination,' ed. Peter M. Haas, *International Organization* 46 (Winter 1992): 1–35.

Hall, Budd L. 'Looking Back, Looking Forward: Reflections on the Origins of the International Participatory Research Network and the Participatory Research Group in Toronto, Canada.' Unpublished paper prepared for the 8th World Congress on Participatory Action Research, Cartegena, Colombia, n.d.

Hancock, Graham. *Lords of Poverty: The Power, Prestige, and Corruption of the International Aid Business*. London: Macmillan, 1989.

Heclo, Hugh. 'Issue Networks and the Executive Establishment.' In *The New American Political System*, ed. Anthony King, 87–124. Washington, DC: American Enterprise Institute for Public Policy Research, 1978.

Helleiner, Eric. *States and the Reemergence of Global Finance: From Bretton Woods to the 1990s*. Ithaca: Cornell University Press, 1994.

Herman, Robert. 'Identity, Norms, and National Security: The Soviet Foreign Policy Revolution and the End of the Cold War.' In *The Culture of National Security: Norms and Identity in World Politics*, ed. Peter J. Katzenstein, 271–316. New York: Columbia University Press, 1996.

Hirst, Paul, and Grahame Thompson. *Globalization in Question: The International Economy and the Possibilities of Governance*. Cambridge: Polity Press, 1996.

Inglehart, Ronald. 'Postmaterialist Values and the Erosion of Institutional Authority.' In *Why People Don't Trust Government*, ed. Joseph S. Nye, Philip D. Zelikow, and David C. King, 217–36. Cambridge, MA: Harvard University Press, 1997.

International Development Research and Policy Task Force. *Connecting with the World: Priorities for Canadian Internationalism in the Twenty-first Century*. Report of the Task Force, Maurice F. Strong, Chairman. Ottawa and Winnipeg: International Development Research Centre, International Institute for Sustainable Development, North-South Institute, 1996.

Irwin, Michael H.K. 'Banking on Poverty: An Insider's Look at World Bank.' In *Fifty Years Is Enough: The Case against the World Bank and the International Monetary Fund*, ed. Kevin Danaher, 152–60. Boston: South End Press, 1994.

Keck, Margaret, and Kathryn Sikkink. *Activists beyond Borders: Advocacy Networks in International Politics*. Ithaca: Cornell University Press, 1998.

Kim, Daniel H. 'Managerial Practice Fields: Infrastructures of a Learning Organization.' In *Learning Organizations: Developing Cultures for Tomorrow's Workplace*, ed. Sarita Chawla and John Renesch, 350–63. Portland: Productivity Press, 1995.

Lindquist, Evert. 'Public Managers and Policy Communities: Learning to Meet New Challenges.' *Canadian Public Administration* 35 (Summer 1991): 127–59.

Lipnack, Jessica, and Jeffrey Stamps. *The Networking Book: People Connecting with People*. New York: Routledge and Kegan Paul, 1986.

Lipschutz, Ronnie D. 'Reconstructing World Politics: The Emergence of Global Civil Society.' *Millennium* 21(Winter 1992): 389–420.

Lipschutz, Ronnie D, with Judith Mayer. *Global Civil Society and Global Environmental Governance*. New York: State University of New York Press, 1996.

Marin, Bernd, and Renate Mayntz, eds. *Policy Networks: Empirical Evidence and Theoretical Considerations*. Boulder/Frankfurt: Westview/Verlag, 1991.

McQuaig, Linda. *The Cult of Impotence: Selling the Myth of Powerlessness in the Global Economy*. Toronto: Viking, 1998.

Mendelson, Sarah. 'Internal Battles and External Wars: Politics, Learning, and the Soviet Withdrawal from Afghanistan.' *World Politics* 45 (April 1993): 327–60.

– *Changing Course: Ideas, Politics, and the Soviet Withdrawal from Afghanistan*. Princeton: Princeton University Press, 1998.

Naisbitt, John. *Megatrends Asia: Eight Asian Megatrends that Are Reshaping Our World*. New York: Simon and Schuster, 1996.

Nevitte, Neil. *The Decline of Deference*. Peterborough, ON: Broadview, 1996.

Nye, Joseph S., Philip D. Zelikow, and David C. King, eds. *Why People Don't Trust Government*. Cambridge, MA: Harvard University Press, 1997.

Pauly, Louis. 'Capital Mobility, State Autonomy, and Political Legitimacy.' *Journal of International Affairs* 48 (Winter 1995): 369–88.

Peattie, Lisa. 'Urban Research in the 1990s.' In *Preparing for the Urban Future: Global Pressures and Local Forces*, ed. Michael A. Cohen, Blair Ruble, Joseph Tulchin, and Allison Garland, 371–91. Washington, DC: Woodrow Wilson Center Press, 1996.

Powell, Walter W. 'Neither Market nor Hierarchy: Network Forms of Organization.' *Organizational Behavior* 12 (1990): 295–336.

Putnam, Robert. *Making Democracy Work: Civic Traditions in Modern Italy.* Princeton: Princeton University Press, 1993.

– 'Bowling Alone: America's Declining Social Capital.' *Journal of Democracy* 6 (Jan. 1995): 65–78.

– 'Tuning In, Tuning Out: The Strange Disappearance of Social Capital in America.' *PS: Political Science and Politics* 28 (Dec. 1995): 664–83.

Putnam, Robert D., Susan J. Pharr, and Russell J. Dalton. 'Introduction: What's Troubling the Trilateral Democracies?' In *Disaffected Democracies: What's Troubling the Trilateral Countries?* ed. Susan J. Pharr and Robert D. Putnam, 3–30. Princeton: Princeton University Press, 2000.

Ranis, Gustav. 'The World Bank near the Turn of the Century.' In *Global Development Fifty Years after Bretton Woods: Essays in Honour of Gerald K. Helleiner,* ed. Roy Culpeper, Albert Berry, and Frances Stewart, 72–89. London: Macmillan, 1997.

Reinicke, Wolfgang, and Francis Deng. *Critical Choices: The United Nations, Networks, and the Future of Global Governance.* Ottawa: IDRC, 2000.

Richardson, Karen. 'Seeking Peace through Scientific Exchange.' *The Medical Post,* 5 August 1997.

Risse-Kappen, Thomas. 'Ideas Do Not Float Freely: Transnational Coalitions, Domestic Structures, and the End of the Cold War.' *International Organization* 48 (Spring 1994): 185–214.

Rosenau, James N. *Along the Domestic Foreign Frontier: Exploring Governance in a Turbulent World.* Cambridge: Cambridge University Press, 1997.

Schon, Donald. *The Reflective Practitioner: How Professionals Think in Action.* New York: Basic Books, 1983.

Senge, Peter. *The Fifth Discipline: The Art and Practice of the Learning Organization.* New York: Doubleday, 1991.

Shaw, Martin. *Global Society and International Relations.* Cambridge: Polity, 1994.

Siegel-Itzkovich, Judy. 'Canadian MDs Help Heal Middle East Wounds.' *The Jerusalem Post,* 16 March 1997.

Sikkink, Kathryn. 'Human Rights, Principled Issue Networks, and Sovereignty in Latin America.' *International Organization* 47 (Summer 1993): 411–41.

Stren, Richard. 'Urban Research and Urban Researchers in Developing Countries.' *International Social Science Journal* 48 (March 1996): 107–19.

– 'Research on Urban Governance in the Developing World: Toward a New Approach to Comparative Operational Knowledge.' Paper presented to the APPAM Conference, Pittsburgh, 1 November 1996.

Swartz, David. *Culture and Power: The Sociology of Pierre Bourdieu.* Chicago: University of Chicago Press, 1997.

Tesher, Ellie. 'Helping Kids Know No Boundaries.' *The Toronto Star*, 21 April 1997.

Wapner, Paul. 'Politics beyond the State: Environmental Activism and World Civic Politics.' *World Politics* 47 (April 1995): 311–40.

Wellman, Barry, ed. *Networks in the Global Village.* Boulder: Westview Press, 1999.

Wellman, Barry, and S.D. Berkowitz. 'Toward a Structural Sociology.' In *Social Structures: A Network Approach*, ed. Barry Wellman and S.D. Berkowitz, 1–18. Cambridge: Cambridge University Press, 1988.

Wolfensohn, James D. 'The World Bank and the Evolving Challenges of Development.' Speech given in Washington, DC, 16 May 1997. Available on the Internet from the World Bank's home page: www.worldbank.org.

World Bank. *World Development Report 1998: Knowledge for Development.* Washington, DC: World Bank, 1998.

Index